JANE'S POCKET BOOK 19
HEAVY AUTOMATIC WEAPONS

JANE'S POCKET BOOK 19
HEAVY AUTOMATIC WEAPONS

Edited by Denis Archer

MACDONALD AND JANE'S

FIRST PUBLISHED 1978

ISBN 0354 01141 3 (PVC EDITION)
ISBN 0354 01140 5 (LIBRARY EDITION)

Printed in Great Britain by
Netherwood, Dalton and Co. Ltd.,
Huddersfield

PUBLISHED BY MACDONALD AND JANE'S PUBLISHERS LTD.
PAULTON HOUSE, 8 SHEPHERDESS WALK, LONDON N1 7LW

CONTENTS

FOREWORD

In common with others in the series this pocket book is designed to meet the needs of those who require a readily-portable digest of weapon information or for whose purposes the larger *Jane's* yearbooks, with their wider and more detailed coverage, are inappropriate.

This volume is primarily concerned with guns which can be used by soldiers to perform tasks which are generally beyond the capabilities of a light machine gun but less demanding than those for which guns customarily classified as artillery are usually employed. All the weapons here described are 'automatic', in the sense of being self-loading at least, but can in normal use be manually aimed and fired at a visible target.

Scope

These definitions, however, are inadequate as criteria for making a unique selection of weapons for inclusion in the book. At one end of the range of possible candidates, for example, there are numerous sustained-fire variants of rifle-calibre light (or 'general-purpose') machine guns which, suitably mounted, can perform a variety of functions not significantly less extensive than those for which a purpose-built medium machine gun is suitable — although the more rugged construction of the latter may give it a longer life in such roles. Although this book is in the main complementary to *Jane's Pocket Book of Rifles and Light Machine Guns,* therefore, there is some overlap between the heavier weapons described in that book and the lighter weapons described in this and the adjective 'heavy' in the title is to be regarded as relative rather than absolute.

Among the heavier weapons described here are several which have been incorporated in elaborate systems in which the processes of target detection, identification and engagement are considerably aided by radar, optoelectronics, computers, servomechanisms and so forth. Such systems, most of which are designed primarily for use against aircraft, are important and increasingly common features of the military scene; and brief descriptions of such special mountings — including some naval versions which may upon occasion be used by soldiers or marines — have been incorporated with the entries for the guns that are used in them. No attempt has been made, however, to describe the target acquisition and fire control systems in detail. In selecting vehicle mountings for description, moreover, emphasis has been placed on those used on lighter vehicles. A machine-gun mounted in the elaborate turret of a main battle tank is not a negligible weapon, but its importance in relation to the tank's main armament is scarcely such as to justify a description of the turret as a whole in this book.

Many of the heavier weapons described were originally developed for use on aircraft or naval vessels; but while the similarity between some naval mountings and those

Left: *Effect of intense cannon fire on a tank. This sequence of pictures shows the destructive capability of the GAU-8/A 30 mm cannon carried by the USAF/Fairchild A-10 close-support aircraft.* Above: *A remotely controlled naval anti-aircraft weapon system—the Breda Twin 40/70 Compact—comprises two 40 mm Bofors L/70 guns and an elaborate automatic feed system, all of which is remotely controlled*

designed for use by land forces makes it reasonable to include references to such mountings here — indicatively rather than exhaustively — to attempt to cover the wide range of special aircraft mountings would be inappropriate to the main purpose of the book. There are, moreover, some airborne weapons, of the same general nature as some of those described here, which have not yet been used in any weapon system for land forces and these too have been excluded. An important example is the formidable General Electric GAU-8/A 30 mm gun which is installed in the USAF/Fairchild A-10 close-support aircraft and which has a rate of fire of 4,200 rounds per minute and a muzzle velocity of 1,060 metres per second. It may be noted, however, that this weapon is one of several being considered in connection with the US Army Radar/Gun Air Defence System (ARGADS) requirement.

For similar reasons, naval weapons not used by land forces have been excluded, as also have remotely-controlled unmanned naval mountings even though they may contain guns which are described in the book. Finally there are a few very heavy automatic weapons — such as the Bofors 155 mm self-propelled automatic gun — which clearly belong in the artillery category.

At the end of all this, however, there inevitably remains an arbitrary element in the selection process and it would be unrealistic to expect my choice to be acceptable to all. Much the same can also be said both of the older weapons

described in this book and of those that are not yet in service: several virtually obsolete weapons have been included because there is some evidence to show that they are still in service somewhere in the world and some new projects have been excluded because the available information is too sketchy to be worth recording;

Status

For most weapons some indication of present status is given. In this context 'present' covers a period extending roughly from the Autumn of 1976 to the Spring of 1977; but news travels slowly in some channels and some of the information may be older than these dates suggest.

Data

In order to keep entries reasonably short I have confined the tabulated data to a few significant characteristics which vary slightly with weapon type. Dimensions have been limited to major items and are expressed (except for calibres which are given in imperial or metric units according to custom) only in metric units. For the smaller weapons dimensions are given to the nearest 0.5 centimetre in length and 0.1 kilogram in weight: less precise figures are given for the larger weapons.

The Bofors SP 155 mm gun fires automatically and is fed with clips containing 14 rounds of ammunition—each round weighing some 85 kg. It can fire at up to 15 rounds per minute

Arrangement

Weapons and their mountings have been arranged in ascending order of weapon calibre, in alphabetical order of country of origin within each calibre division and roughly in chronological order within each country subdivision. For the few weapons that have been made in more than one calibre the main entry will be found under the most familiar calibre (or the smallest calibre if there is no other preference) and a note has been made at the beginning of each other relevant calibre division.

Where a weapon is or has been manufactured under licence or copied in a country other than its country of origin, a separate entry for the licence-built version or copy is included only if it is noticeably different from the original or otherwise of special importance. If a separate entry is not thus justified the details of known licences and copies are given in the main entry for the weapon.

Mountings developed in one country for use with weapons developed in a different country are, with a few exceptions, described in the country subdivision appropriate to the mounting and a cross-reference is incorporated in the weapon description.

Finally there is an index which, it is hoped, will resolve any difficulties which these notes on arrangement have not elucidated.

Denis Archer

11

INTRODUCTION

Military commanders have always been interested in ways of increasing the firepower of their forces; and when gunpowder became known to the warring nations of Europe, it was not long before efforts were devoted to the problem of increasing the number of projectiles that could be delivered in a given period of time.

The practice of putting a number of muskets together on a frame or, later, on a cart and firing them in succession, was frequently adopted; but the difficulty of reloading in the face of an active enemy and the physical effort involved in moving the assembly encouraged the search for a more practical arrangement. Several weapons resulted from this search, all of dubious value and all accorded an undue amount of publicity. The most famous was undoubtedly Puckle's Gun which was, essentially, a large flint-lock revolver on a very modern-looking tripod. The cylinder was rotated by hand and lined up with the barrel; and a half turn of the handle behind it screwed the whole cylinder forward and the tapered end of the chamber entered the barrel and made a gas-tight fit. It was in fact extraordinarily modern in its conception. It was reported in the London Journal of 31 March 1722, that the machine was discharged in the Artillery Fields 63 times in seven minutes. This was accomplished by a single man during a rain storm. The inventor declared his intention of firing round bullets against Christians and square ones against Turks. The plan came to nothing but the weapon is still in the Tower of London as a memorial to a remarkable idea for its time.

The next development was the battery gun evolved during the American Civil War. This differed little from the earlier organ gun in principle and consisted of a series of barrels lying flat on a carriage. The most successful was the Billinghurst Requa Battery Gun which had 25 barrels of .58in (14.7mm) calibre. An open powder train connected the breeches of all 25 barrels and a single percussion cap provided the ignition impulse to fire them in one volley. The barrels could be adjusted for height and spread and the three-man crew was said to be able to fire off seven volleys in a minute. The gun weighed 1,300 pounds (590kg). This type of gun was designed to assist in the defence of bridges which were frequently covered and ideal for the employment of such a weapon.

The Gatling Gun

Another Civil War invention was the Gatling Gun. Whilst the war was in progress Doctor Gatling received no encouragement but, when the fighting stopped, interest started to appear and eventually the weapon was widely adopted throughout the civilised world and lasted well into the 20th century. It had a number of barrels, initially six, arranged on a central axis around which they revolved. The barrels were rotated by hand cranking and the ammunition dropped into place from a hopper. In recent years the Gatling principle has returned to favour in the design of aircraft and anti-aircraft weapons, such as the US Vulcan gun, which use a rotating multi-barrel assembly to give a very high rate of fire. The essential difference between such weapons — often described as Gatling-type guns — and the original is that the mechanical functions in the modern weapon are performed automatically.

Several other hand-operated guns, such as the American Gardner and the Nordenfelt (invented by Heldge Palmcranz) were also widely adopted; but all such weapons became obsolete when Hiram S. Maxim invented the Maxim Gun. This gun differed from all its predecessors in one simple respect: it derived the energy to carry out its cycle of operations, not from the muscular efforts of its operator, but from the propellant itself. This revolutionised the weapons industry and started a train of events that in their consequences have had as much effect on the history of Europe and America as any other single event, including the invention of the atomic weapon.

The Maxim gun was what would now be called a medium, or sustained fire machine gun. The First World War saw the development of the light machine gun, carried by one man and served by one other. It also saw the heavy machine gun, of first .5in and then 20mm calibre, develop into a reliable and practical weapon for use in tanks or on aeroplanes and eventually in anti-tank and anti-aircraft roles.

The principles employed in the design of automatic weapons were established before the end of the 19th century. Maxim covered nearly all the possible approaches in a series of patent applications, many of which have been taken into use. Some of them still remain to be exploited but almost all the big discoveries were made early on, and since then the improvements have largely been due to the improved knowledge of metallurgy and the use of improved and lightened materials. It is still the deficiencies in materials used that prevent improvements in weapon design that are long overdue. For example the most pressing problem has always been that of heat dissipation from the machine gun barrel. The effect of undue heat accumulation is to degrade the barrel steel and to reduce its physical strength until erosion of the softened material has enlarged the bore to the extent that accuracy is no longer obtainable and eventually safety is impaired.

Modern Weapons

Maxim solved the heat problem for the first generation of machine guns by using water cooling and surrounding the barrel with a jacket. This was effective but it made the gun heavy, water was sometimes difficult to obtain and the system produced a revealing plume of steam when used for sustained fire. Modern guns, using cartridges of the same calibre, have the same basic heat problem; but the desire for light and highly mobile equipment has led to the adoption of air cooling in place of water cooling. This change, however, has resulted in a considerable loss of firepower; whereas the Browning, Maxim and Vickers guns of the First World War were all capable of about 10,000 rounds an hour for extended periods of time — depending in fact almost entirely on the back-up they received in ammunition and barrels — the modern machine gun can barely provide one-third of this volume of fire at greatly reduced range. The reason is simply that the machine gun is no longer as uniquely important as it was. The mortar, the light support gun, the tank and the aircraft have effects which are not confined to rear areas; they can also be used in the immediate battle, and as a result the role of at least those machine guns which use rifle-calibre ammunition has been significantly reduced in importance. For certain special — and notably anti-aircraft — applications, however, there has been a considerable increase in the deployment of multiple mountings for the smaller-calibre weapons and of weapons with calibres of 20mm or more.

External Power

Most of the weapons described in this book derive the power needed to extract and eject the spent cartridge case and reload and recock the weapon from the effects of the combustion process in the chamber — either by using the mechanical recoil effect or by using some of the propellant gas to drive the working parts to the rear. Most of them, too, use percussion-fired ammunition, the primer of which is mechanically detonated by a firing pin associated with the bolt mechanism. There are a few weapons, however, most of which are required to produce high and accurately-controlled rates of fire, in which some or all of the operations of unloading, loading and firing are powered from an external source. Examples are the Vulcan gun, mentioned above, whose rotating barrel assembly is driven by an external motor, the Hughes chain guns, which have rotating bolt assemblies which are externally powered, and the French M621 cannon which is electrically powered and fired.

Standardisation

A brief glance at the contents of this book will show that there is a very wide range of types and calibres of ammunition for automatic weapons in service today. As most readers will know, there has for many years been considerable agitation within the NATO alliance for a greater degree of standardisation of weapons and ammunition and it is probable that any NATO decisions in this respect will be followed by many other countries. Currently, however, the emphasis is more on the smaller calibres of ammunition; and there is no immediate prospect of a change that will affect more than a handful of the weapons described here.

WEAPONS WITH CALIBRES LESS THAN 7.62mm

Note. Although it is now almost certain that the countries of the NATO alliance will, in the course of the next few years, decide to adopt a standard calibre, for rifles and light machine-guns, of less than 7.62mm, and although their example is likely to be followed by many other countries, it is by no means certain that there will be a similar reduction in calibre for heavier weapons.

Of the two weapons described here, one — the French 7.5mm AA 52 GPMG — is also made in 7.62mm calibre as the AA 7.62 N-F1 GPMG which is described, together with various special mountings (which can also be used for the 7.5mm version) among the 7.62mm × 51 weapons: the other is the American 5.56mm XM-214 which is a lightweight version of the 7.62mm M134 Minigun which in turn is a derivative of the 20mm M168 gun used in the Vulcan air defence system.

Weapons made primarily for use in 7.62mm or larger calibres (and therefore described later in the book) are:

7.62mm (× 51) FN MAG made in 6.5mm as the Swedish M58 GPMG. Most of these have been converted to 7.62mm calibre which is now a standard in the Swedish armed forces.

7.62mm (× 51 or × 39) Heckler and Koch HK 21 series also available in 5.56mm calibre.

After World War II the French Army had no modern weapons of native design but was equipped with a variety of British, American and German guns. This diversity of weapons and the difficulty of supplying spare parts contributed to their disaster in Indo-China.

The Arme Automatique Transformable Model 52 — GPMG model 1952 — fires the French 7.5mm × 54 cartridge of 1929. A version firing the 7.62mm × 51 cartridge is also made and known as AA 7.62 N-F1. For both versions there is a choice of light and heavy barrels. It is a blowback-operated weapon, firing from an open breech and using a two-part breech-block with a delaying lever action to prevent premature opening of the breech while the chamber pressure is high. The chamber has a fluted neck to permit gas to flow round the outside of the cartridge, thus easing extraction.

Cartridge head space is critical and provision is made for the rapid replacement of the bearing surface in the receiver. In spite of this the ejected cases are deformed where they expand into the bullet guide. Any relaxation of case manufacturing tolerances could result in a blow-out.

The AA 52 uses a French disintegrating link belt based on the US M13. The AA 7.62 N-F1 can use either this type of belt or the M13 — NATO belt. Unlike the FN MAG the AA 52

7.5 mm AA 52 GPMG with heavy barrel

must be carried with the gun cocked when a loaded belt is in place.

Ammunition: 7.5mm M/29 (or 7.62mm NATO)
Operation: Delayed blowback
Feed: Disintegrating link belt (see text)
Sights: Slit blade foresight, 200-2,000 metres leaf rear.
Weight: With light barrel, bipod and flash hider 10.0kg: with heavy barrel 11.4kg
Length: With light barrel and butt extended 114.5cm: with butt retracted 98cm: with heavy barrel and butt extended 124.5cm
Rate of fire: Cyclic 700 rounds/min; Practical (heavy barrel) 250-500 rounds/min; (light barrel) 150 rounds/min
Practical range: Heavy barrel 1200m; light barrel 800m
Maximum effective: 3,000m
Manufacturer: GIAT — Originally developed and produced by Manufacture Nationale d'Armes de Chatellerault (MAC). Production subsequently transferred to Manufacture Nationale d'Armes de Tulle
Status: Production complete for 7.5mm version. Adopted by the French Army and still probably in service in some former French colonies. Now superseded in production by the 7.62mm version. The 7.5mm calibre is still used in Switzerland.

The success of the M134 Minigun (qv) has led GE to produce a lightweight version in 5.56mm intended for use in vehicles, small boats, or emplaced on the ground. It is similar in general arrangement to the M134 but several design innovations have been made including an access cover lever/safing lever which allows the gun to be made incapable of firing when the lever is in the "safe" position.

The XM 214 has been produced in a complete lightweight system intended for use on the M122 tripod or from a vehicle. The system with 1,000 rounds of ammunition weighs some 39kg and consists of three major components, the XM214 gun, the ammunition package, and the power module.

Linked ammunition is stored in 500-round cassettes and two cassettes are held in the ready for use position on the ammunition rack. When the gun is firing the feeder pulls ammunition to the gun from the front cassette through a length of flexible chuting. When the first cassette is emptied, ammunition is supplied from the second cassette and this trips a visual warning system, indicating to the gunner the need to add another cassette.

The power module contains the 24V plug-in battery and the motor together with the solid-state electronic controls.

The battery is nickel-cadmium, is rechargeable in 15 minutes, will fire 3,000 rounds from one charge and has a life of over 1,000 recharges.

The solid-state printed circuit panel in the power module controls the burst-limit, firing rate and automatic clearing of the gun.

Ammunition: 5.56mm × 45
Operation: Battery powered, air cooled
Feed: Linked belt
Fire: Automatic. One of two selected rates between 400 and 4,000 rounds/min
Sights: telescopic.
Weights:
Complete system (including 1,000 rounds): 38.6kg
Gun: 12.2kg
Lengths:
Overall: 104cm
Gun: 68.5cm
Width (including ammunition case): 44.5cm
Manufacturer: General Electric (USA)
Status: Evaluation

5.56 mm XM-214 gun

7.62mm (× 51) CALIBRE WEAPONS

Note. Three types of 7.62mm ammunition are commonly used for medium machine-guns. In terms of numbers of different types of weapon the most common cartridge is the 7.62mm × 51 NATO round: the larger 7.62mm × 54R rimless round is used by Russian forces and by those of her satellite and client countries. The third 7.62mm round is better known as the US .30-06 and is used in the Browning machine guns: a fourth is the Russian 7.62mm × 39 which is used in lighter weapons.

This division of the book deals with weapons chambered for the 7.62mm × 51 round and the next two divisions deal with the 7.62mm × 54R and the .30-06. Weapons firing the 7.62mm × 39 rounds are not separately described but it may be noted that the Heckler and Koch (Germany — BRD) HK21 series can be supplied in this calibre.

One version of the Czech Model 59 GPMG is chambered for the NATO round and is designated VZ59T. The other versions are made for the 7.62mm × 54R and the weapon is described in that calibre division.

Right: *FN MAG 58*

The FN MAG is gas-operated and belt-fed and has a quick-change barrel. It is light enough to be carried by infantrymen and is capable of producing sustained fire over considerable periods when mounted on a tripod.

It is a sturdy reliable gun with a regulator which will allow the weapon to function well and overcome adverse operating conditions. It fires the standard NATO 7.62mm cartridge from a disintegrating link belt of the US M13 type; alternatively the 50-round continuous articulated belt can be used but the two types of belt are not interchangeable. It has been made in other calibres — notably

for Sweden in a calibre of 6.5mm for the M58 GPMG. In its MMG role the gun can be mounted either on a FN spring-buffered tripod or on one of the range of Danish DISA (Dansk Industri Syndikat A/S) AA field or vehicle mountings. The UK versions of the weapon have their own mountings which are separately described.

The gun has a long-stroke piston-operated mechanism, gas being tapped for this purpose from a point towards the muzzle end of the barrel and fed into a regulator which has a surrounding sleeve inside which is a gas plug with three gas escape holes. When the gun is clean and cold most of the gas passes out through these three holes and only the minimum required to operate the gun passes back to the piston head. As the need arises to increase the gas pressure to overcome the frictional resistance caused by the expansion of heated components, gas fouling or the ingress of sand etc., the gas regulator knob is rotated, the gas regulator sleeve slides along the gas block and the three holes are progressively closed until eventually all the gas is diverted to the piston head. This same arrangement can be used to vary the rate of fire within the limits of 600 to 1,000 rounds a minute.

A co-axial version of the gun is available for AFV mountings. One use is as secondary armament in the turret of the AIFV purchased by the Netherlands from FMC in the USA (see 25mm calibre weapons) and another is in the turret of the Belgian Leopard tanks.

Ammunition: 7.62mm × 51
Operation: Gas, automatic
Feed: Belt
Weight: Gun (without butt or bipod) 10.1kg; with butt and bipod 10.8kg; 50-round belt 1.5kg
Length: Gun (with flash suppressor) 125.5cm; barrel 54.5cm
Sights: Blade foresight. Leaf rearsight 200-800m aperture (flat) 800-1,800m U-notch (raised)
Rate of fire: 600-1,000 rounds/min cyclic; 250 rounds/min practical
Effective range: 1,200 metres
FN TRIPOD
Weight: 10.5 kg
Maximum height of barrel axis: 72cm
Minimum height of barrel axis: 25.5cm
Total traverse: 67°
Total elevation: 30°
Manufacturer: Fabrique Nationale, Herstal
Status: In production. In service with forces of Argentina, Belgium, Cuba, Ecuador, India, Israel, Kuwait, Libya, Netherlands, New Zealand, Peru, Qatar, Rhodesia, Sierra Leone, South Africa, Sweden, Tanganyika, Uganda, Venezuela and elsewhere. Additional data on the UK versions are given separately.

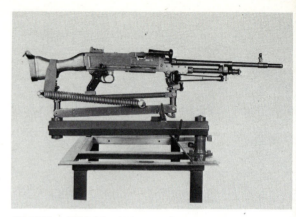

FN MAG on DISA AA vehicle mounting

On the MG version of the FN 4RM/62F AB light armoured car there is a twin mounting for 7.62mm GPMG. This is a turret mounting, the relatively large turret accommodating commander and gunner and being electrically traversed. The commander's cupola has eight periscopes and the gunner has three periscopes and a sight. Each man has a hatch cover opening to the rear.

In addition to the two MG the turret is armed with a 60mm grenade launcher which can be elevated independently to 75 degrees. The guns can be elevated to 55 degrees and all weapons depressed to −10 degrees. Elevation is manual. 7.62mm ammunition capacity is 4,380 rounds.

Another version of the same vehicle has a 90mm CATI gun as its main armament. Associated with this, in a turret similar to that of the MG version is a coaxial version of the GPMG and a standard version is mounted outside the commander's cupola for AA defence.

Manufacturer: FN, Herstal
Status: Production complete. In service with the Belgian Gendarmerie. No other known sales.

Madsen-Saetter GPMG

DENMARK

MADSEN-SAETTER GPMG

This GPMG was the last of the Madsen series of machine guns and was introduced in the 1950s. Since then the makers of the series, Dansk Industri Syndikat AS, have ceased making weapons, although they still make machine gun mountings. The gun is gas-operated with a simple locking system involving a lug on each side being forced out of the bolt and into recesses in the receiver. It is, unfortunately, possible to assemble and fire the gun with the lugs missing.

The weapon was a contender in the British GPMG trials in 1958 but did not there prove itself to be reliable. It came into the field rather too late and the cream of the market was taken by FN. It was made in limited numbers at the Bandung arsenal in Indonesia.

It is no longer in production. A prototype .5 version was produced but this was never put on the market.

Ammunition: 7.62mm × 51
Operation: Gas, automatic
Feed: Belt. Usually 50 rounds. Continuous links but can be modified for disintegrating links
Weight: 10.1kg
Length: 97cm: Barrel 56.5cm
Sights: Blade foresight, tangent notch rear
Rate of Fire: Cyclic 750 rounds/min; Automatic 200 rounds/min
Effective range: 800 metres
Manufacturer: Dansk Industri Syndikat AS-(DISA). (Also made in Indonesia).
Status: No longer manufactured. No longer in European service. Locally manufactured weapons in service in Indonesia.

AA 7.62 N-F1 GPMG

This is the version in 7.62mm × 51 calibre of the 7.5mm AA 52 weapon, described earlier, which it has superseded in production. It is generally similar to the earlier weapon and is available in ground, AFV and aircraft-mounting versions. For ground use it can be mounted on a tripod and various mountings are available for vehicle use: there is also a version with a heavy barrel and without stock or sights for coaxial mounting on armoured vehicles.

Ammunition: 7.62mm × 51
Operation: Delayed blowback, automatic
Feed: Disintegrating-link or continuous link belt
Weight: (heavy barrel version) 10.6kg without mounting. Tripod 10.6kg
Length: 124.5cm (butt extended); 108cm (butt retracted)
Sights: Folding foresight; 200-2,000m graduated rear sight
Rate of fire: 900 rounds/min cyclic; 250-300 rounds/min practical
Effective range: About 800m
Manufacturer: GIAT
Status: Production and service in the French Army at least.

CB 52 V VEHICLE MOUNTING

This Creusot-Loire mounting is suitable for use with the 7.62mm N—F1 (or 7.5mm AA 52) GPMG. It has been adopted by the French Army for use in a close defence role on the VAB front-armoured vehicle but can be used in a similar role on many other transport or combat vehicles.

The mounting consists of a rotating shield which carries the gun and an ammunition box and is suitably manoeuvrable for the engagement of ground and air targets. Mounted over a hole in the top of the vehicle and level with the firer's shoulders the mounting is provided with folding half doors which can be closed to provide NBC protection without removing the gun.

Weapon: 7.62mm × 51 or 7.5mm GPMG
Traverse: Unlimited
Elevation: Either −15° to +45° or +20° to +80° with shield locked in either case.
Weight: Mounting only, 132kg; Weapon 10kg; Ammunition box (full) 8kg; Total 150kg
Mounting hole diameter: 63cm or 70.5cm
Manufacturer: Creusot-Loire

Creusot-Loire CB mounting for 7.62 mm MG

MASCOT VEHICLE MOUNTING

GIAT Mascot mounting

Designed for close-in defence, the Mascot is a 7.62mm GPMG mounting which can be fitted either on a mounting plate integral with the vehicle as a ring mounting or in a rotating cast body having all-round vision periscopes and an access hatch. For the simpler arrangement a round or square aperture 48.5cm is required: the more elaborate version rides on an 83cm diameter ball-race.

The weapon mount acts as a protective casing for the optical system which comprises two mirrors with sight lines etched on them: an X3 magnification telescope may be added. A standard 200-round ammunition box is carried on the mount and a feed belt stop system provides for recharging: the weapon may thus be aimed, fired and reloaded with the firer under cover.

Power for the simpler mounting is supplied directly by cable; and in this configuration traverse is not unlimited. For the more elaborate mounting a wiper ring is built into the ball bearing assembly. Elevation limits are −13° to +50° for both versions.

Manufacturer: GIAT
Status: In production. An optional tear gas grenade launcher will be available.

TLi.52A LIGHT CUPOLA

This is a close-in defence GPMG mounting (7.62mm or 7.5mm) for use with transport and combat vehicles. Mounted on top of the vehicle level with the firer's head it provides light armour and NBC protection during firing.

The cupola is fitted with a coaxial-pattern MG and a range of optical devices. These comprise a unit magnification episcope and oscillating head prism associated with a X5 magnification binocular, 6 lateral fixed episcopes and a searchlight coupled to the weapon support. An extractor fan is provided and power is supplied through a rotating joint in the cupola bearing.

Traverse: Unlimited
Elevation: −12° to +45°
Weight: 150kg with weapon and ammunition
Mounting hole diameter: 63cm or 70.5cm
Cupola base diameter: 80cm
Height: 32cm
Manufacturer: Creusot-Loire
Status: Prototype.

Creusot-Loire TLi.52A light cupola

This cupola provides a mounting for a GPMG (7.62mm or 7.5mm) and a 40mm grenade launcher and can be mounted on transport or combat vehicles for close-in defence use. Mounted on the roof of the vehicle, level with the firer's shoulders, it provides light armour and NBC protection during firing.

The mounting is fitted with a coaxial-pattern MG and a 40mm rifle grenade launcher, and optionally with a smoke-bomb launcher, and a range of optical devices comprising a unit magnification episcope assembly and a searchlight coupled to the weapon support and 4 lateral fixed episcopes. An extractor fan is fitted.

Traverse: Unlimited
Elevation: −13° to +55°
Weight: 300kg with weapons and ammunition
Mounting hole diameter: 70.5cm
Manufacturer: Creusot-Loire
Status: Production

TLi.52G cupola

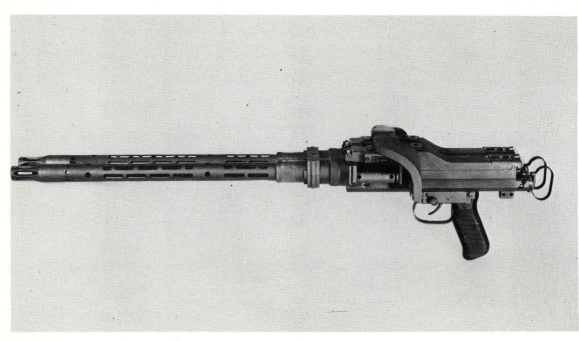

During the Second World War Mauser-Werke at Obern-dorf produced the MG81 in 7.92mm. It was designed initially for aircraft use and, to increase its fire power, was built as a twin-barrelled machine gun (MG81Z) with one common receiver and trigger. This twin-barrelled gun produced 1,700 to 1,800 rounds/min/barrel. Three such twin-barrelled guns were used in an additional pod attached to a Ju 88 or Do 217. In some cases as many as 6 pods were attached to a Ju 88 giving a fire power of 60,000 rounds/min.

The lack of penetration of the 7.92mm bullet led to the development of larger calibre machine guns and the MG81 was used for airfield defence and installed on S-boats for AA protection. About 200,000 MG81s were made. Many were equipped with a shoulder stock and sights and used as ground machine guns.

After Germany came into NATO Mauser resurrected the MG81 rebuilt to 7.62mm × 51 NATO. The gun was aimed first at the helicopter market where the value of a fast-firing light machine gun would be appreciated. With a twin-barrelled MG81Z on each side of the helicopter the pilot would have a fire power of 6,800-7,000 rounds/min. The second possibility was to use the gun in the ground role with a reduced rate of fire of 1,200 rounds/min.

Mauser twin-barrelled MG81Z

The gun is very light and occupies little space and operates, in principle, in the same way as the 7.92mm MG34 (qv) with a rotating bolt head. The recoil action is the same but rather a lot of gas assistance is used at the muzzle.

Ammunition: 7.62mm × 51
Operation: Short recoil with gas assistance, automatic
Feed: Either disintegrating link belt or 100-round continuous belt

Weights:	MG81	MG81Z
(helicopter version):	6.5kg	12.9kg
(ground role):	8.5kg	—
Length		
(incl. flash hider):	94cm	94cm
Barrel:	47.5cm	47.5cm
Distance between bores:	—	5.5cm
Sights:		
Foresight:	Pillar	Pillar
Rearsight:	Notch	Notch
Rate of fire:		
(helicopter version):	1,700 rds/min	3,400 rds/min
(ground version):	1,200 rds/min	

Effective Range: 800 metres
Manufacturer: Mauser-Werke
Status: Available for production.

HECKLER AND KOCH HK21 SERIES GPMG

HK21 is a belt-fed GPMG designed to use the 7.62mm × 51 NATO cartridge but capable of being converted to fire the 5.56mm × 45 or 7.62mm × 39 rounds. Normally used with a disintegrating link belt, which may be the German DM6 or the French or US (M13) belts, it may also be used with the DM1 continuous-link belt.

Essentially a light machine gun, it is suitable for a sustained-fire role by virtue of its quick-change barrel and by the availability of a range of special mountings. The principle of operation is delayed blowback, using the two-part breech-block and roller delay system which is used in the G3 automatic rifle and a fluted chamber to ease cartridge extraction. The gun fires from the closed breech position.

Ammunition: 7.62mm × 51 (or 5.56mm × 45 or 7.62mm × 39
Operation: Delayed blowback, automatic
Feed: Belt
Weight: Gun (without bipod) 7.3kg; vehicle version 7.1kg
Barrel: 1.7kg
Bipod: 0.6kg
Length: 102cm (with butt); vehicle version (without butt) 82cm; barrel 45cm
Sights: Blade foresight; aperture drum rear. Clicks every 100 metres. Adjustable for windage. 200-1,200 metres
Effective range: (7.62mm × 51) 1,200 metres
Rate of fire: 900 rounds/min. cyclic: Practical (2 barrels) 200 rounds/min
Manufacturer: Heckler and Koch
Status: In production. In service with Portuguese Army and in various African states and S.E. Asia.

Heckler and Koch belt-fed HK21 GPMG

HECKLER AND KOCH HK21A1 GPMG

This is a further development of the HK21 which incorporates a fold-down feed mechanism. This arrangement makes the task of loading the gun easier and simplifies belt removal and the rectification of stoppages.

HK21A1 mounted on a 1200-series tripod, which is simpler and more rugged than the 1100-series

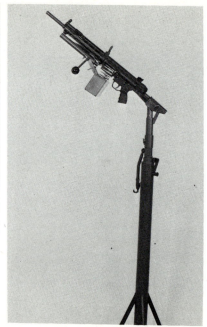

Above: *HK21A1 on the 1100 tripod.* Right: *2400-series column mount*

Heckler and Koch have developed several mountings for their HK 21 series MG and similar weapons. There are the Tripod Mount 1100 and a series of vehicle mountings described separately below. All are available and cradles for MG other than the HK21 series can be supplied.

TRIPOD MOUNT 1100

This is a spring buffered tripod which can be folded and carried into action on the shoulders of one man. When set up its height (measured as bore centre line above ground) can be adjusted between 35cm and 75cm. The rear legs of the tripod can be folded to allow use in a small weapon pit.

There is a 43 degree traversing arc between the two rear legs and the rear attachment of the gun to the arc is by the elevating column which permits an elevation of 14 degrees. The elevating column can rapidly be disconnected to allow a 360 degrees traverse of the gun.

Attached to the elevating column housing is a dial sight with a periscope optical viewing eye piece. The sight can be levelled by spirit level and, by reference to an aiming mark, it can be used to engage targets, the bearing and elevation of which have been previously recorded after ranging.

The sight also allows the gunner to produce traversing fire between set stops on the traversing arc, and searching fire.

Traverse (on arc): 43°
Elevation: 14°
Folded dimensions: 77cm long, 57cm wide and 23cm high
Weight: 9.2kg

COLUMN MOUNT 2400

This mount is intended for use on a light vehicle. It is a spring balanced system and with the butt of the weapon replaced by a receiver end cap, the weapon can be traversed rapidly and elevated up to 75 degrees or depressed to −15 degrees. The amount of traverse varies with the type of vehicle and the restrictions imposed by vehicle design, but with an open vehicle, the gun can get 90 degrees of fire on either side whilst the vehicle is moving.

The same mounting can be used for a static anti-aircraft defence system

ANTI-AIRCRAFT / GROUND MOUNT 2700

This system is designed for use with armoured vehicles having a top hatch. The weapon can be rotated rapidly through 360 degrees and from −10 degrees up to 75 degrees. At any point it can be locked in position for the engagement of ground targets.

The gun is used without the buttstock and is so mounted that no turning moments are produced when firing.

CIRCULAR TRACK MOUNT

This mount is designed to go on unarmoured load-carrying vehicles. It can be fitted above the passenger seat in the cab of a lorry and allows the gun to deal with either ground or air targets.

The circular track rotates throughout 360 degrees and allows rapid traverse. When it is locked in position the gun has a traverse of some 180 degrees and can be elevated from −15 degrees to +75 degrees. The buttstock is removed and the rear of the gun is supported in prolongation of the barrel axis. Thus there is no turning moment when the gun is firing. The 100-round belt is located in a box below the gun. To use the HK21 in a dismounted role, the gun can be disengaged from the mounting, the buttstock fitted and the bipod positioned quickly.

Weight: 33.5kg
Outside diameter: 76cm
Inside diameter: 64.5cm
Diameter of hole: 72.5cm
Height of mount above roof: 31cm
Height with gun fitted: 32.5cm

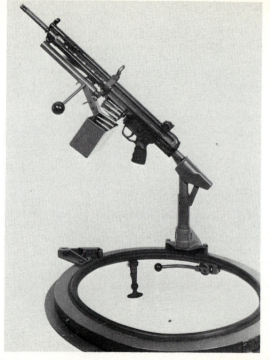

Right: HK Circular Track Mount. Far Right: *AA fire position of the 2700-series AA/Ground mount*

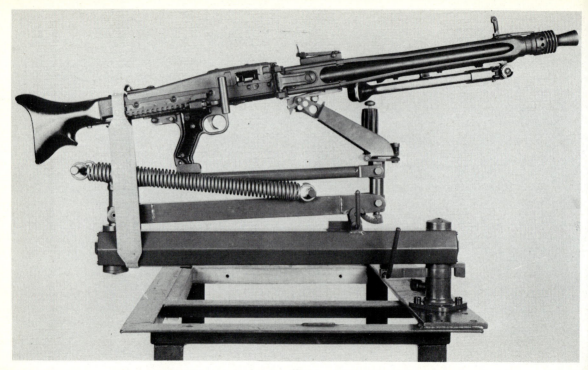

This weapon is a derivative of the highly successful Second World War weapon which was first used in action in the Western Desert in 1942 and was subsequently used on every battle front where the German Army was in action. The weapon's post-war history is complicated but the following brief summary covers most of the details which are relevant to weapons which are or may be still in service.

When the German forces came into NATO they decided to modify the MG42 design from 7.92mm calibre to 7.62mm × 51 and adopt it as their standard General Purpose Machine Gun. It was manufactured by Rheinmetall in 1959 and called by them the MG42/59. The Bundeswehr called it the MG1. The earliest MG1 fired the 7.92mm × 57: the MG1A1 was chambered for the 7.62mm × 51 contained in a continuous belt and the barrel was chrome plated. The MG1A2 could be fed from the German 50 round continuous belt known as the DM1 or the US M13 disintegrating link belt: the MG1A3 had some small changes intended to speed production including the rounded muzzle booster and will only fire the continuous belt.

In parallel with this development process, some of the original MG42 weapons were converted from 7.92 to 7.62

MG42 on DISA AA vehicle mounting

calibre and were redesignated MG2. The current weapon, however, is a further development known as the MG3 which came into service in 1968; it has the external shape of the MG1A3 and can be fed from the German DM1 continuous belt or either the German DM6 or the US disintegrating link belts. It has an AA sight and a belt retaining pawl to hold the belt up to the gun when the top cover plate is lifted.

The original MG42 was used by the French Army for several years until the AA52 came into service. The Yugoslav Army uses a gun called the SARAC M1953, which fires the German 7.92mm × 57 wartime cartridge in the DM1 belt, and is still manufactured in Yugoslavia. The MG42/59 is used by Austria, Denmark, Spain (where it is made under licence at Oviedo), Chile, Turkey, Iran and Pakistan (where it is manufactured as the MG1A3). It is manufactured in Germany for the Bundeswehr. In Italy it is manufactured by a consortium of Beretta, Luigi Franchi, and Whitehead Moto Fides. Beretta makes the bolts, Franchi the barrels and Whitehead the trigger mechanisms. The guns are assembled by Beretta and Whitehead.

The disintegrating link belt of the US M13 or the German DM6 type can be used in the MG1A2 or the MG3. It is factory filled and is not intended to be refilled after use. The continuous belts of the German DM1 type which are the only type used in the SARAC M53, the MG42, MG1 and MG1A3, and can also be used in the MG1A2 and MG3, can

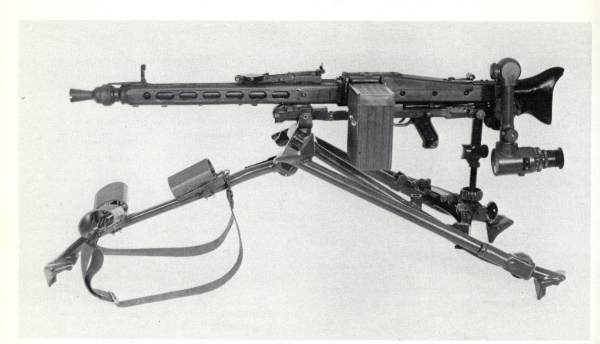

be refilled after use.

The gun operates on the short recoil principle, using a roller locking system which functions as a bolt accelerator in the recoil phase. The recoil forces are enhanced by a muzzle booster.

In its original form the MG42 fired at about 1,200 rounds a minute and the standard bolt used in the MG1A1, MG1A3 and the MG3 weighs 550g and produces this rate of fire. The MG1A2 uses a heavy bolt weighing 950g and this produces rates of about 900 rounds a minute. The German Army uses the lighter bolt but the Italian MG42/59 uses the heavier bolt. If another rate of fire were required this could be obtained by changing the bolt, buffer spring or muzzle booster appropriately.

Firing in short bursts at a rate of about 200-250 rounds a minute, the barrel should be changed after 150 rounds, ie three 50-round lengths. The barrel change is very quick and simple.

A buffered tripod to allow sustained fire is available and can be fitted with a dial sight allowing engagement of unseen targets and recording of previously registered targets.

The MG3 is used in both coaxial and AA mountings in the Leopard tank family and in German reconnaissance vehicles.

Ammunition: 7.62mm × 51
Operation: Short recoil, automatic
Feed: Belt
Weight: Gun without bipod 10.5kg; Bipod 0.5kg; Barrel 1.8kg
Length: 109.5cm without butt; 122.5cm with butt; Barrel with extension 56.5cm; Barrel without extension 53cm
Sights: Barleycorn foresight, notch rear, folding AA sight
Rate of fire: 700-1,300 rounds/min cyclic; 250 rounds/min automatic
Effective range: 800m from bipod; 2,200m from tripod
Manufacturer: Rheinmetall
Status: In production in Germany. Also produced in Italy by Beretta, Luigi Franchi and Whitehead Moto-Fides, and in Spain, Portugal and Pakistan. Also in service with the forces of Austria, Denmark, Chile, Turkey, Iran, Norway and the Sudan and in Leopard tanks in Australia, Denmark, Germany, Italy, the Netherlands and Norway. Belgian Leopard tanks are fitted with the FN MAG 58. MG42 produced in Yugoslavia as SARAC M1953.

MG3 on Heckler and Koch 1100-series tripod

Several vehicle mountings have been developed for the MG3. Three examples of those currently in service in the German armed forces are described briefly below

On the Radspähpanzer 2 Luchs reconnaissance vehicle there is a ring mounting for the standard version of the MG over the commander's hatch. The main armament of the vehicle is a 20mm cannon and this has an infra-red/white searchlight coupled to it. There is no independent light source for the MG3 which is moved independently by hand with elevation limits of −15 to +55 degrees an unlimited traverse.

On the Marder M1CV there are two MG3 mountings. One is of the weapon modified for coaxial mounting with the 20mm Rheinmetall Rh 202 cannon. The two weapons are mounted in a turret described later with other Rh 202 mountings.

At the rear of the Marder hull roof is a (Mowag pattern) remotely-controlled MG3 mounting with a traverse of 180 degrees and elevation limits of −15 to +60 degrees.

Vehicle Manufacturer: Rheinstahl, Kassel (both) and Atlas Mak. Kiel (Marder)
Status: Both vehicles are in service with the German Army.

The remotely-controlled MG3 mounting can be seen mounted at the rear of the Marder MICV

This gun started as the model 9M and was accepted into service with the Japanese Self-Defence Force in 1962. It has a reputation for reliability and accuracy.

The locking system is very unusual in that it is a tilting block with the front of the bolt forced up by cams on the piston extension (slide) to lock. Two wings level with the centre line move into recesses in the receiver and the bolt is held in position by the piston extension under it. The final movement of the piston, after locking is completed, carries the firing pin, fixed to the piston post, through the block, into the cartridge cap. Until the front of the block has risen there is no hole for the firing pin.

After the round has fired, some of the propellant gas passes through the gas port and drives the piston to the rear. The firing pin is withdrawn and the front of the bolt is first cammed down and then pulled back.

The extraction is also unusual. There is no spring-loaded extractor hook but whilst the round is in the chamber, before firing, there is a spring-loaded plunger forced up into the cannelure from below. When the front end of the bolt is carried down, a fixed hook on the bolt face above the firing pin hole, drops down and grips the cannelure of the cartridge head. When the bolt starts back the case is withdrawn.

The barrel retaining catch is depressed by lifting the top cover plate. The carrying handle is rotated and then the barrel can be pushed forward. Whilst the top cover plate is lifted it prevents the front of the bolt from rising into the locked position and so the firing pin hole is blocked. This prevents the feed and firing of a round when this is unlocked or there is no barrel in position.

Ammunition: 7.62mm × 51
Operation: Gas, automatic
Feed: Disintegrating-link belt
Weight: 10.7kg; barrel 2.0kg
Length: 120cm; barrel 63.5cm
Sights: Blade foresight, leaf aperture rear. Cranked telescopic sight.
Rate of fire: 550 rounds/min cyclic
Effective range: 600m from bipod; 1,100m from tripod
Manufacturer: Nittoku Metal Industry Co
Status: In production and in service with the JSDF. A coaxial version is mounted on the Type 74 main battle tank.

M62 GPMG

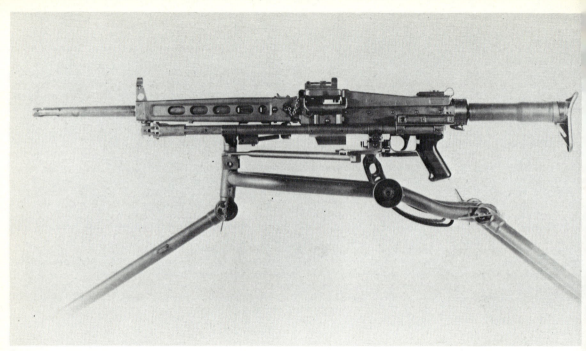

Tripod-mounted SIG 710-3 GP MG

This is a delayed-blowback weapon employing a roller delay mechanism and a fluted chamber to ease extraction of the spent case. As with many other delayed-blowback mechanisms the breech block has two major operating parts; the rear part being accelerated with respect to the forepart as the rollers are disengaged from the body of the gun. It is unusual, however, in having a third part in the form of a sleeve round the rear part: during the forward movement of the mechanism this component is still travelling forwards when the cartridge cap is struck, thus preventing the bolt from bouncing in the event of a slight hangfire and providing a small additional delay by virtue of its forward momentum.

The gun is belt-fed and can use either the German continuous-link belt or disintegrating-link belts of the US M13 pattern with a simple change of feed tray and cartridge guide. The feed energy is adequate to lift a belt 1.2 metres long. A heavy barrel is available for sustained-fire operations and the barrel change is simple.

The standard tripod for the gun is the SIG L810 which is a sprung tripod with provision for automatic fire dispersal in train, elevation or both.

Ammunition: 7.62mm × 51
Operation: Delayed blowback, automatic
Feed: Disintegrating link or continuous-link belt
Weight: 9.3kg with bipod and standard barrel. Add 0.5kg for heavy barrel, and 0.8kg for belt carrier (not used in sustained-fire role).
Length: 114.5cm; barrel 56cm
Sights: Blade foresight; leaf notch rear 100-1,200m in 100m steps ×2.5 telescopic sight available.
Rate of fire: 600 rounds/min cyclic; 200 rounds/min automatic
Effective range: 800m from bipod; 2,200m from tripod
TRIPOD TYPE L810
Firing height: 30.5cm min; 70cm max
Weight: 10.3kg
Maximum elevation: 28°
Maximum traverse: 45°
Dimensions folded: 82 × 46 × 27cm
Weight of telescope and mount: 1.85kg
Manufacturer: SIG
Status: Available

Two types of remotely controlled 7.62mm MG mounting have been used on various models of the Mowag armoured vehicle series and one, an enclosed mounting, has been employed also in various versions on vehicles made in other countries — notably on the Marder MICV described above among the German entries. The other is an open mounting, shown as one of the armament options for the 4 × 4 Piranha APC but its present status is not known.

The enclosed mounting is to be found on the 8 × 8 Piranha APC, the Tornado MICV and some of its variants and the Taifun MICV from which the Tifone MICV has been developed in Italy by Oto Melara. As specified for the Tornado, the mounting comprises the MG, in an enclosed box mounted on trunnions which form part of a rotatable turret assembly, and optical and control equipment. The turret, which is controlled entirely from within the vehicle, is provided with two vision blocks and a PERI Z12 sighting telescope. Elevation limits for the gun are −15 to +60 degrees: traverse varies according to the nature of the installation and is 230 degrees for the Tornado.
Vehicle Manufacturer: Mowag Motorwagenfabrik AG
Status: Enclosed mounting in service in Germany at least.

Left: *Two MOWAG remotely-controlled MG mountings can be seen at the rear of this Tornado MICV.* Far left: *Note the muzzle-brake blast of the 20 mm cannon*

This weapon, currently the standard GPMG of the British armed forces, is a close derivative of the Belgian FN MAG (qv). The decision to use the Belgian weapon as the basis of the British GPMG programme following the adoption of the 7.62mm × 51 round by NATO was taken after a series of trials in 1957 and a slightly modified version of the MAG

was made at RSAF Enfield and put into service as the L7A1 in 1961. Service experience, however, indicated the need for further minor modifications and the resulting weapon was designated L7A2.

In its general principles of operation the L7A2 is indistinguishable from the FN MAG. A parallel development of a tripod for the sustained fire role of the weapon, however, led to the L4A1 tripod which differs considerably from the FN tripod on which the MAG is normally mounted for sustained fire from the ground. Although developed primarily for the British weapon, this tripod design is basically suitable for use with all similar weapons and the RSAF have produced similar mountings adapted for use with a wide variety of other machine guns.

Ammunition: 7.62mm × 51
Operation: Gas, automatic
Feed: Belt
Weight: Gun with bipod 10.9kg; Barrel 2.7kg
Length: 123cm
Sights: Blade foresight. Aperture rear graduated 200-800 and 800-1,800m
Rate of fire: 750-1,000 rounds/min cyclic. 100-200 rounds/min automatic
Effective range: 1,200m
Manufacturer: Royal Small Arms Factory, Enfield
Status: Production complete. In service with British forces.

Left: *L7A2 arranged as a helicopter door gun. Note the trigger arrangement.* (JSPRS, Singapore). Above: *L7A2 mounted on a pulk for use in the snow* (HQ UKLF PR)

This is a derivative of the British L7 GPMG which was developed, after consideration of other possibilities, as a replacement for the 7.92mm BESA, the weapon derived from the Czech Model 37 which had been the standard British tank gun in the Second World War.

The L7 GPMG can be fed only from the left; its gas system is of the 'exhaust to atmosphere' type, and to remove the belt from the gun it is necessary to lift the top cover plate, housing the feed mechanism.

All these factors make it unsuitable for tank use. The necessity to feed from the left dictates the position of a coaxial machine gun relative to the main armament and this is not always the position the designer or the user would prefer.

Any gas-operated gun releases fumes to the immediate surrounding area through gas vents and the 'exhaust to atmosphere' system is particularly bad because when the gun is operating under the most favourable conditions the amount of gas escaping through the regulator is at its greatest.

The interior of a tank turret can be very cramped and the machine gun may have to be mounted with insufficient clearance to allow the top cover plate to be lifted sufficiently to allow the belt to be removed. The ideal gun has its hinges along both sides of the upper surface of the receiver so that the cover requires the minimum overhead clearance and can be opened to either side.

The L8 machine gun embodies the necessary changes to improve the L7 for tank use but embodies the same basic design features. The gas regulator plug has three radial gas ports of increasing diameter and fits into a conical seating to eliminate any gas leakage. Also to exclude gas from the interior of the AFV, the usual gas escape holes are omitted from the gas cylinder. Since a feature of this weapon is the exchangeable barrel requirement, the inevitable small escape of gas via the close clearance fit of the gas plug in the front end of the gas cylinder is dealt with by a fume extractor tube fitted into the conical flash suppressor and led back to the regulator spindle nut. The gases emerging from the muzzle pass the forward end of the excess gas tube and create an area of low pressure, thus sucking out any gas in the tube originating in the gas plug.

Ammunition: 7.62mm × 51
Operation: Gas, automatic, normally controlled by electric solenoid trigger
Feed: Belt
Weight: Gun 10.4kg; Barrel 3.1kg
Length: 110cm
Rate of fire: 650-1,000 rounds/min cyclic
Manufacturer: Royal Small Arms Factory, Enfield
Status: In production and in service with British-built AFV

L37A1 TANK MG

This is a derivative of the L8 Tank MG which can be used in many kinds of AFV but which can also be used dismounted in a ground role by a simple exchange of parts.

To achieve this the gun is made up of a combination of L8 and L7 components. The L8 gun body assembly is the basis of the design but is modified by the addition of an aperture rear sight and the incorporation of the L7 (manual) trigger assembly. For vehicle use the L8 gun barrel assembly (which has no foresight) is normally used but an L7 barrel can be fitted in place of this for ground use, and the addition of a butt and bipod completes the transformation.

Manufacturer: Royal Small Arms Factory, Enfield
Status: In service.

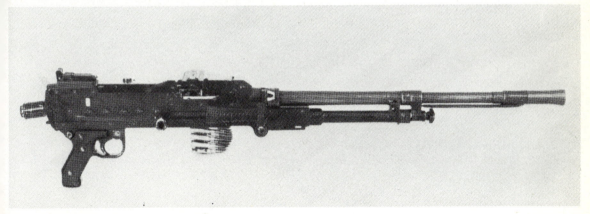

The L37A1 Tank MG is a derivative of the L8A1

L20A1 MG

This gun is a modification of the L8 Tank Machine Gun to enable it to be used in a helicopter. The trigger is electrically controlled, there is no sighting system and the barrel does not have the flash hider and gas tubes of the L3A2 barrel. It has the gas system of that barrel but uses a prong type flash eliminator. The gun can be fed from either side by changing the feed cover with the feed pawls and feed arm and the feed plate.

A duct is installed to convey the expended links into a bag.

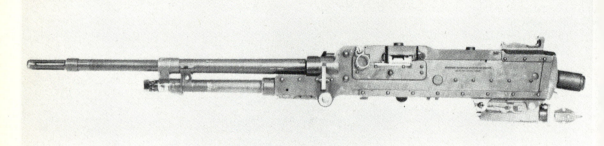

The 7.62 mm L20A1 MG with right-hand feed (RMCS)

Coaxial MG (which can be seen above the driver's head) in the Scorpion turret is the L43A1 used both for ranging the 76 mm gun and as secondary armament

Until very recently it had not been possible to combine the role of the ranging tank machine gun with that of the co-axial machine gun. To some extent barrel wear suffered by the co-axial MG resulted in loss of consistency, essential to a ranging gun, but in addition a problem existed with the movement of the MPI (mean point of impact) of a group of shots from a cold to a hot gun. This was critical since effective ranging is essential with the gun either cold or hot. The L43A1, with its barrel bearing, was an L8 derivative specially developed to reduce this MPI shift to an acceptable level. This bearing is located between the gas block and the muzzle, and supports the barrel at the forward end. The L43A1 does not have the flash hider and gas tube of the L3A2 barrel used on the L8 MG.

Manufacturer: Royal Small Arms Factory, Enfield
Status: In service as a ranging MG on the Scorpion AFV.

Left: *FV 107 Scimitar reconnaissance vehicle in Norway. The gun to the right of the Rarden cannon is the L8A1 Tank MG.* (Sgt J. F. Clark, UKLF PR). Above: *AFV Cupola No 16, developed for the Spartan APC, incorporates a mounting for a GPMG which can be loaded, cocked, aimed and fired from within the vehicle. The arrangement shown here is a prototype*

Typical mountings for the 7.62mm L7/L8 MG and their derivatives described above are briefly noted below.

Chieftain MBT: This has a coaxial L8A1 MG mounted in the turret with the 120mm gun. An L37A1 MG is mounted on the commander's cupola and can be fired from within the cupola.

FV 101 Scorpion: This has an L43A1 ranging MG mounted in the turret with the 76mm gun. It can be used as secondary armament in addition to its ranging role.

FV 107 Scimitar: In addition to the 30mm Rarden cannon this vehicle carries an L8A1 MG in the turret as secondary armament.

Fox Armoured Car: This also is armed with the Rarden cannon and the L8A1 coaxial MG but the turret differs from that of the Scimitar. The same turret is, however, also mounted on a version of the FV 432 APC used by Mechanised Infantry Battalions.

FV 432 APC: Among the many variants of this vehicle is one which carries twin L7 series MG (with ammunition belt boxes) on an open mounting on the commander's cupola for anti-aircraft operations.

Status: All mountings listed above are in service, some of them in many parts of the world.

This is currently the standard GPMG of the US Army and has replaced the .30 Browning MMG (qv) in most US applications although the older weapon is still extensively used by other countries. The M60 is a gas-operated weapon, firing 7.62mm NATO ammunition from a disintegrating-link belt, and its design owes much to that of the German MG42 of the Second World War. The gas system uses the constant-volume principle whereby the unregulated gas supply is cut off by the piston when it completes the short stroke required to drive the working parts to the rear.

When the M60 is used in the sustained fire role the M122 tripod is employed. This is made up of the tripod assembly, the traversing and elevating gear and the pintle and platform group.

The tripod assembly consists of the tripod head and pintle bush and lock, one front leg and two rear legs. The traversing bar connects the two rear legs and supports the elevating and traversing mechanisms.

The M60 uses the M4 pedestal mount for the M151 quarter-ton truck (Jeep). The M142 gun mount (part of the M4 mount) which serves as a cradle for the gun can be used in other vehicles. It has a platform identical to that in the M122 tripod mount.

Ammunition: 7.62mm × 51
Operation: Gas, self-regulating, automatic
Feed: Disintegrating-link belt
Weight: 10.5kg; Barrel 3.7kg
Length: 110cm; Barrel (excluding flash hider) 56cm
Sights: Blade foresight, leaf aperture rear 200-1,200m × 100m
Rate of fire: 550 rounds/min cyclic; 200 rounds/min automatic
Effective range: 800m from bipod, 1,800 from tripod, maximum 3,100m

TRIPOD M122
Weight: 6.8kg
Length: 82.5cm extended; 68.5cm folded
Height: 36cm
Traversing range: 50° or unlimited
Elevating range: −12.6° to +14° locked or −28.8° to +28.5° free
Manufacturer: Bridge Tool & Die Manufacturing Company. Inland Manufacturing Division, General Motors. Maremont Corporation.
Status: Manufacture completed. In service with US forces and in Australia, Taiwan and Vietnam.

Jeep-mounted M60 in the foreground. The soldiers are British Life Guards on a visit to the USA (British Army PR)

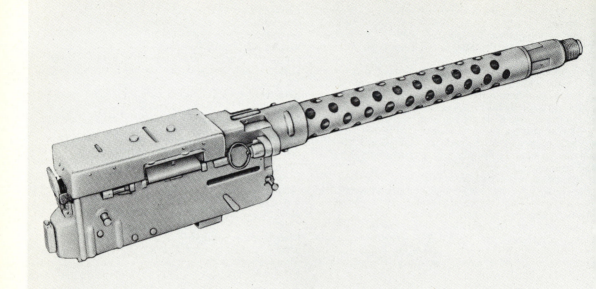

This purpose-built tank MG had several novel features in the design of its mechanism, one being a small sliding breech block with a separate rammer. When the barrel recoiled a lug under the block ran in a cam path in the receiver and the breech block moved over to the right. In this way a short inboard length was obtained: however, with no reciprocating bolt, extraction was complicated and the case was withdrawn by an extractor which transferred it to a carrier which moved back and then rotated down so that the case lay nose forwards under the breech block. When the rammer drove the next round into the chamber it forced the case off the carrier and into a bag. The kinematic path of the empty case was viewed with suspicion when the gun was initially produced, and the gun was first modified as the M73A1 and then replaced by the M219 (qv).

As with the German MG34 tank MG, the receiver of the gun could be rotated with the barrel casing locked into the mantlet, so that the barrel could be withdrawn straight to the rear; and the top cover was hinged on either side to reduce overhead space and allow adjustments to be carried out inside the turret.

The rate of fire was kept down to 500-600 rounds a minute. This slow rate meant that the breech block was slow in opening and so the amount of fumes brought into the crew compartment was minimal. The gun normally fired from the left but could be converted to right hand feed.

Although primarily intended for use as a coaxial gun the M73 could be converted for use on the ground by the addition of a bipod, a pistol grip and a trigger linkage.

Ammunition: 7.62mm × 51
Operation: Short recoil with gas assistance, automatic
Feed: Disintegrating-link belt
Weight: 14kg; barrel 2.4kg
Length: 89cm
Rate of fire: 500-625 rounds/min cyclic
Effective range: 900m
Manufacturer: General Electric (USA). Rock Island Arsenal
Status: No longer in production. Still in service.

M73 Tank MG

M219 TANK MG   (USA)

As noted in the description of the M73 Tank MG, the M219 design was arrived at by a process of necessary modification, and the change of designation was decided upon only because of the extent to which this process had been carried. The M219 is very similar in appearance to the earlier weapon but apparently similar parts are not necessarily interchangeable.

The M219 is slightly lighter than the M73 but the weapon characteristics are similar.

Status: In service with the US Army.

MG nearest to the camera is a M60 GPMG on a shielded mounting. Vehicle is an M113A1 seen in Vietnam (US Army)

There is a very wide range of US AFV mountings for the M60 and tank MG and other weapons, such as the FN MAG, of the same general type. Some of the important ones are listed below.

Tank mountings: The M60 series MBT and the M551 Sheridan light tank have coaxially-mounted M73 MG. Earlier tanks used .30 calibre weapons in equivalent positions.

Lynx Command and Reconnaissance Vehicle: Among the variants of this vehicle offered by FMC are two with cupolas for 7.62mm M73/M219 or .30 MG. The Model 74 Cupola mounts two such weapons and the M113-type cupola, which mounts one, is the alternative.

M114 Command and Reconnaissance Vehicle: This is an example of a vehicle on which the M142 mounting for the M60 GPMG is used.

XM723 MICV: The turret for this FMC vehicle, expected to enter production in 1978/79, carries a coaxial M60E2 MG as secondary armament. The turret is power-operated and stabilised so that weapons can be fired on the move and is provided with day and night sights.

FMC AIFV: The turrets of the AIFV being supplied to the Netherlands by FMC are armed with a 25mm Oerlikon

cannon and a coaxial FN MAG. The turret is fully powered and equipped with a range of day and night observation and firing devices.

Cadillac Gage Commando Series: The many versions of the vehicles in this series include several with twin mountings in turrets and single mountings for a variety of MG including the M60 and M73/M219 weapons.

Secondary armament of this XM 723 MICV prototype is a 7.62 mm MG. Main armament of production models will ultimately be a 25 mm cannon, but the vehicle shown here has a 20 mm cannon

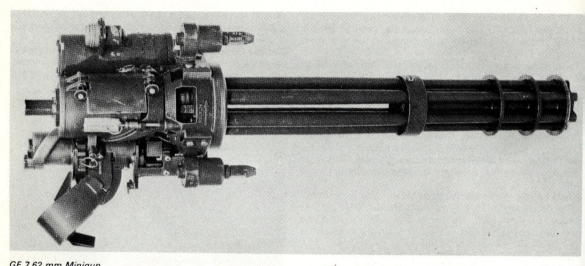

GE 7.62 mm Minigun

This is a six-barrel externally-powered Gatling-type gun developed by General Electric as a smaller-calibre derivative of the 20mm Vulcan gun (qv).

The six barrels and six associated bolt mechanisms are mounted on a rotor which is driven by a 28V electric motor. As the rotor rotates, the movement of each bolt is controlled by an elliptical cam path cut in the inner surface of the stationary gun housing, and as each bolt moves up and down its bolt track a triggering cam controls the movement of the associated firing pin. These movements together enable each bolt mechanism to accept, chamber, lock, fire and extract a cartridge supplied by the ammunition feed. The whole firing and extraction sequence is thus independent of the forces generated when the cartridge fires and a misfire will not cause the mechanism to stop. Ammunition is supplied from a box, which normally has a capacity of 4,000 rounds, by way of a plastic chute.

Ammunition: 7.62mm × 51
Operation: External power, automatic
Method of feed: Linked belt or linkless
Weight: Basic gun 15.9kg; Drive motor 3.4kg; Recoil adapters (2) 1.4kg; Barrel (6) 1.1˙kg each; Feeder 4.8kg
Length: 80cm; Barrel 56cm
Sights: Vary with employment
Rate of fire: Up to 6,000 rounds/min
Manufacturer: General Electric (USA)
Status: In production. In service.

7.62mm CHAIN GUN

Hughes Helicopters and Ordnance Systems have developed a 7.62mm version of their well-known 30mm Chain Gun. The latter weapon is described later in the book and the following notes deal only with the state of progress of the 7.62mm weapon at mid-1977.

At that time some 250,000 rounds had been fired by two prototype weapons, the first firing having taken place in May 1975. These firings included turret firings (5,000 rounds), firing under field conditions (20,000 rounds) an 11,000-round burst with a water-jacketed barrel, 10,000 rounds of 'foreign' ammunition fired without stoppage or malfunction and over 100,000 rounds fired from the first prototype with only one broken part.

The gun is physically interchangeable with the coaxial weapon used in M-48 and M-60 tanks and is envisaged by the manufacturers as appropriate to future US armoured vehicles from APC's to main battle tanks.

Manufacturers: Hughes Helicopters and Ordnance Systems, Culver City, California
Status: Originally a private venture development; now the subject of a US government contract calling for prototype deliveries in 1978.

DUAL FEED ARMOUR MACHINE GUN

Maremount Dual Feed Armour MG

This tank machine gun was designed by Maremont and developed by them under a contract from the US Weapons Command. The weapon was intended to be a replacement for the M73, M73A1 and the M219 and to be employed in the coaxial role as well as being cupola mounted. If required it can be dismounted and fitted with a shoulder stock and bipod or a tripod.

The gun is short-recoil operated and has a quick-change barrel and a dual ammunition feed. Each of the two belt fed modules can be supplied from either left or right side, utilising common components.

Since the gun may well fire ammunition of differing muzzle impulse, an impulse control device is fitted to the gun which can effectively cope with mounts having spring rates which vary widely in value.

Cartridge: 7.62mm NATO of any type (Ball AP etc) or armour piercing flechette
Operation: Short recoil, automatic
Feed: Dual disintegrating link belt
Length: 87.5cm
Rate of fire: 500-650 rounds/min cyclic; 100 rounds/min sustained
Effective range: 1,000m
Manufacturer: Maremont Corporation
Status: Evaluation.

7.62mm (× 54 R) CALIBRE WEAPONS

Note. The 7.62mm × 54 Russian round, also known as the 7.62mm Moisin Nagant, has been a standard rifle/MG round in Russia for many years and has been adopted by Russia's allies and many client countries. In the Chinese People's Republic the round is designated Type 53.

It is believed that all Chinese MG appropriate to this book are copies of Russian weapons. Those relevant to this calibre division are the Types 57 and 63, corresponding to the Russian SG-43 and SGM MMG respectively. It is not certain that they have been made in China; and as there are no known important differences between the Chinese and Russian weapons and as the latter are described later in the book there is no need to repeat the descriptions here.

It is, however, worth noting that some Chinese AFV mount these weapons in either original or copy form. This applies not only to those AFV that are themselves copies of Russian vehicles but also, probably, to such developments as the Chinese T-62 light tank whose turret is believed to be identical to that of the T-60 (Russian PT-76) in which a coaxial version of the Type 63 MMG (Russian SGMT) is mounted.

This Czechoslovakian machine gun followed the Model 52 LMG which it has now largely replaced. It is somewhat simplified in operation and considerably less complicated to produce. It is a true general purpose machine gun and can fulfil a variety of roles. In most of these it fires the Russian 7.62mm × 54R cartridge. As a squad automatic weapon with a light barrel and bipod or as a light machine gun with a heavy barrel and bipod it is known as the VZ59L.

As a medium machine gun with a heavy barrel and a light tripod it is called the VZ59. This tripod also enables the gun to produce anti-aircraft fire. As a tank coaxial machine gun, fitted with a solenoid, it is referred to as the VZ59T. It is also manufactured to use the NATO 7.62mm × 51 cartridge and is then designated the VZ59N. The different cartridge contour leads to a different chamber and bolt face.

The gun fires only from the open pocket metal non-disintegrating Czech belt. The open pocket allows the Russian rimmed cartridge to be pushed straight through the belt and the advantages obtained by having a push-through feed are clearly demonstrated when comparing this system with the complex arrangements for the Russian PK GPMG.

Gas-operated, the gun has a long-stroke piston mechanism. In the versions using the Russian ammunition there is a 2-position gas regulator: in the version using NATO ammunition, however, a 4-position regulator is fitted.

Ammunition: 7.62mm × 54R (or 7.62mm NATO for VZ59N)
Operation: Gas, automatic
Feed: Belt, open-pocket non-disintegrating
Weight: 8.7kg with bipod; 19.2kg with tripod; Heavy barrel 3.8kg; Belt 1.4kg (50 rounds)
Length: 111.5cm with light barrel; 121.5cm with 69.5cm heavy barrel
Sights: Pillar foresight, V-notch rear 100-2,000m × 100m
Rate of fire: 700-800 rounds/min (ground fire). 1,000 rounds/min (AA) cyclic. Practical sustained rate 350 rounds/min with heavy barrel
Effective range: 1,000m from bipod; 1,500 from tripod; Maximum 4,800m
Tripod:
Barrel height: 30-50cm (ground fire) 144cm (AA)
Maximum elevation: 21.5°
Maximum traverse: 43.2° between stops
Manufacturer: Ceskoslovenska Zbrojovka, Strakonice
Status: Production. In service with Czech armed forces and available in either calibre.

VZ59N GPMG

SKOT-2AP APC. The turret is the same as that fitted on the Russian
BTR-60PB and carries a 14.5 mm KPVT and a 7.62 mm PKT MG

Several mountings for 7.62mm MG are to be found on Czech APC. Brief details are given below.

OT-810: The most common version of this Second World War German-built vehicle has an unshielded mounting for a commander's MG which nowadays is a VZ59.

OT-62 Series: The OT-62B (also known as the Model 2) vehicle, which is used only by the Czech Army, has a small turret for a VZ59T providing elevation limits of −10 to +20 degrees and unlimited traverse. The same turret is fitted to the OT-62D of the Egyptian Army.

OT-64 Series: The original OT-64A (SKOT) was unarmed but in the vehicles made for use in Poland (the development having been collaborative) there is a pedestal mount for a 7.62mm MG. This has elevation limits of −6 to +23.5 degrees and a traverse of 90 degrees. The OT-64B (SKOT 2) is used only by the Polish Army and has a 12.7mm or 7.62mm MG on a pedestal with a curved shield. The OT-64C (1) (or SKOT-2AP or OT-64 Model 3) has a turret identical to that of the Russian BTR-60PB and BTR-40P-2 vehicles. This turret is fully enclosed and is armed with a 14.5mm KPVT and a 7.62mm PKT MG. Further details will be found in the appropriate Russian entries.

Reference should also be made to the Polish TOPAS entry below.

Both the FUG M-1963 and the FUG-70 amphibious scout cars have mountings for 7.62mm MG. The earlier, M-1963, vehicle has a pedestal mount which carries either a Russian SGMB or a Czech VZ59 MG, the latter being installed in vehicles used by Czech forces (designated OT-65). This mount has elevation limits of −6 to +23.5 degrees and provides 90 degrees of traverse.

On the FUG-70 there is a turret which carries a 14.5mm KPVT and a 7.62mm PKT MG. Traverse is unlimited and the elevation limits are −5 to +30 degrees. 2,000 rounds of 7.62mm ammunition are carried in the vehicle. Further details of the turret are given in the 14.5mm calibre division later in the book.

Status: Both vehicles are in service and the FUG-70 is believed to be still in production in the Hungarian state factory.

FUG-70 amphibious scout car

TOPAS 7.62mm APC MOUNTINGS

Some Polish versions of the APC known in Czechoslovakia under the OT designation have TOPAS designations and these carry 7.62mm MG.

TOPAS-2AP: This is a Polish modification of the OT-62 and is fitted with a turret armed with a 14.5mm KPVT and a 7.62mm PKT MG. Elevation limits are −5 to +78 degrees, enabling the weapons to be used against ground and air targets, and traverse is 360 degrees. 2,000 rounds of 7.62mm ammunition are carried. The same turret is used on the OT-64C(2) APC (also known as SKOT 2-AP and OT-64 Model 4).

WPT-TOPAS: This Polish-developed recovery vehicle based on the OT-62 has a pintle-mounted 7.62mm PK MG.

Maxim Model 1910 on Sokolov mount (RMCS)

The earliest models of the Maxim Medium Machine Gun purchased by Imperial Russia were made in England, and it was not until 1905 that manufacture commenced at the Tula Arsenal. The first guns had a bronze jacket and were excessively heavy. In 1910 production started of the steel jacketed model which remained in service until the end of the Second World War and was used in Korea by the Chinese and in Vietnam by the Viet Cong.

The Maxim gun used by the Russians differs from the British and German guns in non-essential details but the Russians did have a mount that was unique. This was known as the Sokolov and remained in service until the gun itself was obsolete. Vast numbers of the Maxim were made and even as late as 1944 270,000 were produced.

Details of the operation of the Maxim gun are given under British Machine Guns.

Status: No longer in service in Warsaw Pact countries, but still to be found in Asian countries at least.

SG43 (RMCS)

The Goryunov MMG is a sturdy, simple and reliable gun. It is gas-operated (with a long-stroke piston), fitted with a variable-track gas regulator and belt-fed. It fires from a wheeled tripod, which can be manhandled or towed by an animal or vehicle, from the Sidorenko-Malinovski tripod or from various vehicle mountings.

The belt used is the standard Russian closed-pocket type holding 250 cartridges. The gun fires at automatic only and the massive barrel and the easy change make it possible to sustain a good rate of fire. There is no dial sight as used in the German or British MMGs of the period. The wheeled mounts incorporate coarse traverse and elevating gears and a fine elevating knob. The mounts have separate lock levers for elevation and traverse which are normally secured before firing but the traverse lock lever can be released so that free traverse through 360 degrees is possible.

The sights are simple and easily adjusted. The foresight is a cylinder mounted between two protectors, and the rear sight is a U notch mounted on a tangent leaf placed upright before firing. It is graduated from 2-23 on the left and 2-20 on the right by 100s. The figures on the right are for use with light bullets Type L or LPS weighing 148 grains (9.6g). Those on the left are for heavy bullets, yellow-tipped, weighing 182gr (11.8g).

Six versions of the gun are known:—

SG43: This has a smooth barrel with no fins at all. It has the cocking handle lying horizontally between the two vertical spade grips of the firing gear.

The sear is attached to the return spring guide. The barrel lock is a simple wedge which comes out to the side. There are no dust covers over the feed and ejection openings.

SG43B: This has a micrometer barrel lock and dust covers over feed and ejection openings.

SGM: This has longitudinal fins and a separate sear housing. Dust covers are on late production models. The cocking handle is on the right hand side of receiver.

SGMT: This is the tank version of SGM with a solenoid on the back plate of the receiver.

SGMB: Similar to SGM but has dust covers over the feed and ejection ports.

Hungarian SG GPMG: This gun has a RPD buttstock with a pistol grip. It has an external resemblance to the PK GPMG but there is no hole in the buttstock and the ejection slot is lozenge shaped rather than rectangular.

The Goryunov guns have been used by Communist countries in Europe and Asia and have been issued to Arab countries in the Middle East.

The Chinese version of the SG43 is known as the Type 53 and the SGMB is called the Type 57 heavy machine gun. The Czech version has the marking Vz43 and the Polish gun is stamped Wz43.

Although as an infantry weapon the SG43/SGM is now

no longer used in Warsaw Pact countries (although it continues to be used elsewhere) there are still many in service in AFV mountings. Important examples are those in the T-54 MBT (but not the T-55), which has one SGMT in the turret and another in the glacis plate, and the PT-76 light amphibious tank, which has a SGMT in the turret. These vehicles are so widely used by allied and present and former client countries of the Soviet Union that the SGMT at least must still be regarded as being in worldwide use.

Pedestal and pintle mountings for the SGMB are to be found on the AT-P armoured tracked artillery tractor and on various versions of the BTR-40, BTR-152, BTR-50 and BTR-60 armoured personnel carriers,

Ammunition: 7.62mm × 54R
Operation: Gas, automatic
Feed: Belt
Weight: 13.6kg; Barrel 4.8kg
Length: 112cm; Barrel 72cm
Sights: See text
Rate of fire: 650 rounds/min cyclic; 250 rounds automatic
Effective range: 1,000m
Status: No longer manufactured in Russia. No longer in service as a dismounted weapon in Warsaw Pact countries but extensively used until recently in the Middle East and Vietnam and still in service in Africa. Copied in China as Types 53 and 57. Very widely used as a tank MG.

Chinese militia training with SG43. Its Chinese designation is Type 57

This MG first came to the notice of US intelligence authorities in mid-1964 and was believed to be the replacement for the obsolescent RP46 Company Machine Gun. Since that time, however, the Russians have modified and improved the basic PK so that it has now supplanted not only the RP46 but also the SGM heavy machine gun. The following versions exist:—

PK: the basic gun with a heavy fluted barrel, feed cover constructed from both machined and stamped components and a plain butt plate. It weighs about 9kg.

PKS: the basic gun mounted on a tripod. The lightweight tripod not only provides a stable mount for long range ground fire, but can also be quickly opened up to elevate the gun for anti-aircraft fire.

PKT: the PK as altered for coaxial installation in an armoured vehicle. The sights, stock, tripod, and trigger mechanism have been removed, a longer heavy barrel is installed, and a solenoid is fitted to the receiver back plate for remote triggering. An emergency manual trigger and safety are fitted.

PKM: a product improved PK, with a lighter, unfluted barrel, the feed cover constructed wholly from stampings, and a hinged butt rest fitted to the butt plate. Excess metal has been removed to reduce the weight to about 8.4kg.

PKMS: PKM mounted on a tripod (similar to the PK).

PKB: The PKM with the tripod, buttstock, and trigger mechanism removed and replaced by twin spade grips and a butterfly trigger similar to those on the SGMB. This gun may be known as the PKMB.

The PK and PKM machine guns are infantry support guns normally fired from their bipod mounts but both versions can be installed in the front firing ports of the Soviet BMP infantry combat vehicle. The PKS is used in the role of a heavy machine gun to provide long range area fire and anti-aircraft fire. The PKT is used in coaxial installations on most modern Soviet tanks and armoured personnel carriers. The PKM, although lighter than the PK, is used in the same role. The PKB (PKMB) is probably used as a pintle mounted gun on older vehicles as a replacement for the SGMB.

The PK machine guns are gas-operated (long-stroke piston) rotary-bolt locked (Kalashnikov system), open-bolt fired, fully automatic, belt fed. The ammunition is fed by non-disintegrating metallic belts: current belts are composed of joined 25-round sections but earlier feed belts were made of one 250-round length. The belts are held either in 250-round ammunition boxes, in special large capacity boxes on tanks (for the PKT) or in a 50-round assault magazine attached to the bottom of the gun's receiver.

Ammunition: 7.62mm × 54R
Operation: Gas, automatic
Feed: Non-disintegrating metallic belt, 50, 100, 200 or 250 rounds
Weight: 9.0kg on bipod; 16.5kg on tripod
Length: Gun 116cm; 126.5cm on tripod; Barrel 66cm
Sights: Cylindrical post foresight, vertical leaf rear
Rate of fire: 650 rounds/min cyclic; 250 rounds/min automatic
Effective range: 1,000m
Status: In production and in service with Russian, allied and client forces.

PKB MMG on BTR-60 APC; that in the foreground being a BTR-60PK

0.30in CALIBRE WEAPONS

Note. 0.30in calibre ammunition, commonly known as .30-06 or 7.62mm × 63, is used in machine guns throughout most of the world; but the weapons relevant to this book in which it is used are only the MG of the US Browning series and the copies thereof that are made in several countries.

A summary of known vehicle mountings — including those developed outside the USA — follows the weapon descriptions.

Browning's water-cooled Model 1917 was the US machine gun of the First World War although the decision to order it in quantity was taken too late for it to see much service. It remained in the inventory until 1936 when several modifications were introduced — one of them being a new tripod — and the modified weapon was designated M1917A1. With little further modification the weapon then remained in service until after the Second World War. It has long been obsolete in the USA but a few weapons are known to remain in service elsewhere. The possibility of making it in 7.62mm × 51 calibre was considered but abandoned in favour of the M60 (qv).

The gun has a short recoil operating principle, bolt and barrel remaining locked for some 8mm rearward travel after firing, after which the breech is unlocked and a mechanical accelerator imparts momentum to the bolt at the expense of that of the barrel. The barrel is surrounded by a water jacket, and the associated piping and condenser can arrangement restrict the circumstances in which it can be satisfactorily used.

Ammunition: .30-06 (7.62mm × 63)
Operation: Short recoil, automatic
Feed: 250-round belt
Weight: Gun complete 18.6kg; Barrel 1.4kg
Length: 98cm; Barrel 60.5cm
Sights: Blade foresight; leaf aperture rear 100-3,400yds × 50 (91-3,109m)
Rate of fire: 450-600 rounds/min cyclic; 250 rounds/min automatic
Effective range: 1,000m. Maximum up to 4,100m according to ammunition type
Manufacturer: Colt's Patent Firearms Manufacturing Company. Remington Arms-Union Metallic Cartridge Co.
Status: No longer manufactured. No longer in service with the army of any major power but a few survive elsewhere — notably in South America.

Browning Model 1917A1 water-cooled MMG

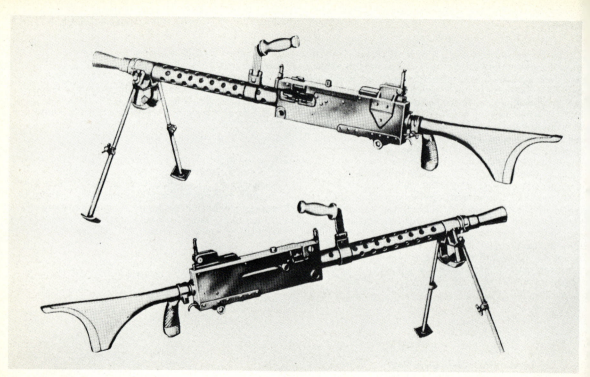

BROWNING MODELS 1919A4 AND 1919A6

To increase the flexibility of the Browning M1917 an air-cooled version was introduced. Its first application was as an aircraft gun, designated M1918, and from this the Browning tank machine gun and subsequently the M1919 dual-purpose weapon were derived.

The mechanism of the M1919A4 is identical with that of the M1917A1. The differences in general design are mainly the replacement of the water jacket by a perforated steel barrel casing, the introduction of a heavier barrel and different sights. Despite the heavier barrel the air-cooled weapon has a rather lower capacity for sustained fire.

Model 1919A4 was used as a fixed gun in tanks in the Second World War and is still in use on many AFV. During the war it was also used as a company MG, mounted on the M2 tripod, with the addition of a flash hider and a detachable carrying handle.

Model 1919A6 is a derivative of the M1919A4 designed primarily for ground use. It has a different flash hider, a lighter barrel, a barrel jacket modified to accept a removable bipod, a removable carrying handle and a removable metal shoulder stock. Apart from these changes and some minor alterations to make the weapon easier to use the design is the same as that of the earlier weapon. Dimensional differences are summarised below.

	M1919A4	M1919A6 (with butt and bipod)
Weight of gun	14.1kg	14.7kg
Weight of barrel	3.3kg	2.1kg
Length of gun	104.5cm	134.5cm

Common Data (where differing from M1917A1)
Sights: Blade foresight, leaf aperture rear of different design
Rate of fire: 400-500 rounds/min cyclic; 120 rounds/min automatic
Effective range: 600m from bipod; 1,000m from tripod
Tripod: M2 weighing 6.4kg
Status: No longer manufactured in USA but possibly still manufactured elsewhere. M1919A4 still in widespread service on AFV mountings but no longer used dismounted in the USA. M1919A6 no longer in US service but likely to be encountered in any country that has received US military aid and many others.

Browning Model 1919A6

.30 BROWNING AFV MOUNTINGS

Vehicle mountings of the .30 Browning weapons and copies thereof are far too numerous to describe even briefly within the compass of this book. Although many of them are on vehicles that have long been obsolete in their countries of origin both vehicles and weapons are still in service, in one form or another, in most of the countries that have received arms supplies from the USA and Western Europe. A highly condensed summary of known mountings believed to be still in service is given below. The weapon in each case is either the US M1919A4 or a locally-built copy of it.

France: Some AMX VCI supplied to Belgium.
Japan: Type 61 Tank (coaxial mounting).
UK: Saracen APC (turret); Ferret, Saladin (coaxial and AA) and some Shorland reconnaissance vehicles; some Centurion tanks (coaxial). Charioteer tank destroyer (coaxial).
USA: Some M113 APC variants; M3A1, M8 and Staghound (coaxial and ball mountings) reconnaissance vehicles; tank mountings for M5, Sherman and M24 (all with coaxial and bow mountings); M41, M47 and some M48 (all with coaxial mountings); and the M36B1 SP ATk gun (bow) and M42 SP AA gun (on gun turret).

Far left: *M706 Commando APC with twin .30 Browning MG in its turret.* Left: *A Browning .30 MG arms the turret of this Saracen APC* (Army PR HQ Northern Ireland)

.303in CALIBRE WEAPONS

Note: .303in (7.7mm) calibre ammunition was for many years a standard for British forces and those of most of the British Empire. It is no longer an important calibre in any major army but it is still extensively used by smaller countries, mainly for rifles and LMG. The Maxim and Vickers machine guns still survive in a few places in this calibre, however, and the Maxim is also still to be found in Russian-made versions (M1910 or SPM) in 7.62mm × 54R calibre or as the Chinese (1935) Type 24 in 7.92mm (Mauser) calibre.

Hiram C. Maxim, an American who came to England in 1881, not only invented but also manufactured the first true machine gun. In 1884 he demonstrated his first model which was a large, heavy, and clumsy piece of equipment some 1.45m long and 1.07m high on its tripod; but the model, although of great technical interest, was never produced. Instead Maxim simplified it, greatly modified the action, lightened it and improved the feed. The production model was ready for demonstration in 1884; and in the same year the Maxim Company was formed.

The gun was demonstrated extensively in 1887 and 1888 in the United Kingdom, Austria, Hungary, Germany, Italy, Russia, Switzerland and the USA. The trials were successful — in spite of many difficulties put in Maxim's way — but orders were slow. The British Government for example purchased three guns and it was not until 1891 that a scale of two guns per battalion was authorised for the regular army.

The Germans and Russians set up manufacturing plants of their own.

Maxim guns were first used in action in the Matabele War of 1893. They were very successful in the Sudan campaign and were employed extensively by both sides in the Boer War. The Russo-Japanese war of 1904 showed the potentialities of the gun but it was in the First World War that the Maxim used by the German Army, and the British Maxim and Vickers — a derivative of the Maxim — were so terribly effective.

In the First World War the Maxim gun was manufactured at the Royal Small Arms Factory at Enfield Lock until 1917.

Ammunition: .303in Mk 7
Operation: Short recoil with toggle joint locking. Automatic fire. Water-cooled.
Feed: 250-round fabric belt
Weight: 18.2kg
Length: 118cm; Barrel 72cm
Sights: Blade foresight. Leaf notch rear
Rate of fire: 600 rounds/min cyclic; 200 rounds/min automatic
Effective range: 2,800m
Manufacturer: Royal Small Arms Factory, Enfield, Middlesex. Also made (in different calibres) in China, Germany and Russia
Status: No longer manufactured. Some British guns probably still survive in various parts of the world. The Chinese version (1935) in 7.92 Mauser calibre is probably still in service as the Type 24 in the Chinese militia: it is a copy of the German Maxim 08 but has a less elaborate tripod mounting. The Russian-made weapon in 7.62mm × 54R calibre (M1910 or SPM) is probably still to be found in Asia: it was used in Vietnam. A rather different version (M/32-33) in the same calibre was used by the Finnish Army in recent years.

VICKERS MK 1 MACHINE GUN   (UNITED KINGDOM)

This was a modified version of the Maxim gun developed by Vickers at Erith. More efficient and lighter than the Maxim but generally similar in operation, it served the British Army well for more than half a century (1912-1968) and was noted for its feats of endurance. It could fire at 10,000 rounds an hour for as long as it could be supplied with water, ammunition and replacement barrels. The barrel was changed every 10,000 rounds and a good detachment rarely took much over two minutes for this task and lost only the water that entered the new barrel as it was pushed in from the rear. Using the Mk 8Z streamlined bullet it could provide deadly, indirect fire on reverse slopes and enemy forming up places as much as 4,500yds (4.1km) away — a feat no NATO machine gun of 7.62mm calibre can accomplish today.

Ammunition: .303 Ball Mk 7 or 8Z
Operation: Short recoil with toggle-joint locking and automatic fire. Water cooled.
Feed: 250-round fabric belt
Weight: 15kg without water; Water 3.2kg; Tripod 22.7kg
Length: 115.5cm; Barrel 72.5cm
Sights: Blade foresight; leaf aperture rear dial sight available
Rate of fire: 450-500 rounds/min cyclic; 125 normal; 200 rapid
Effective range: 4,100m indirect; 3,380m direct
Manufacturer: Vickers, Vickers-Armstrong and Royal Ordnance Factories
Status: No longer manufactured. Still in service in the Middle East and probably in Asia. Used in Pakistan as recently as 1972. A few are still in service with the Royal Marines.

7.92mm (×57) CALIBRE WEAPONS

Note. The 7.92mm × 57 (Mauser) round was a standard German round in the Second World War and was adopted by many other countries in the immediate post-war years. More recently its influence has waned as the major alliances have standardised on 7.62mm rounds; but some very good weapons were made in this calibre and considerable numbers of some of them are still in service.

German Maxim-type MG in this calibre and the copies made elsewhere are discussed in the entry for the .303in British Maxim in the preceding division.

The SARAC M1953 made in Yugoslavia is chambered for this round but is otherwise a copy of the German MG42 (see description of 7.62mm × 51 MG3, Germany).

Left: *.303 Vickers Mk 1 MG with dial sight*

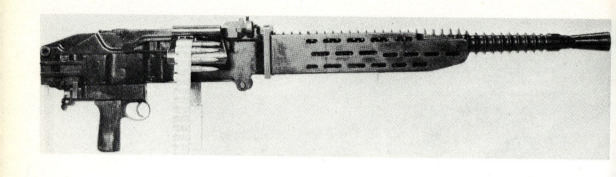

This gun was manufactured from 1937: its nomenclature in the Czech army was the Model 37 and it was sold commercially as the VZ 53.

It was an air-cooled, belt fed gun, gas-operated and very sturdy. The bolt locked to the barrel extension and not into the receiver so that the barrel and block could recoil together within the receiver before unlocking occurred. This was intended to reduce the trunnion pull by dissipating energy before the whole gun recoiled and so reduce the load on the tripod or vehicle mount.

The Model 37 fed from the right and could use either a metal or a fabric-cum-metal continuous open pocket belt. It introduced the cocking system which later was used on Models 52 and 59, in which the trigger mechanism is pushed forward and the sear used to pull the piston and breech block to the rear. This system was used on the British wartime BESA Tank MG and has recently been employed in the Colt CMG-2 LMG.

The Model 37 could be employed on its tripod as a medium machine gun or as an anti-aircraft gun. The German Army used it both as a tripod-mounted MMG and in their tanks as the MG 37(t). It had two rates of fire, a buffer device being interposed to shorten the recoil distance and to return the bolt forward at high speed. Without the device the rate of fire was about 450 rounds/min and with it the rate went up to about 700 rounds/min.

The Czech gun can be distinguished from all but the very earliest British BESA guns (qv) by the perforated side plates of the receiver. The British guns had plain slab sides.

Ammunition: 7.92mm × 57
Operation: Gas with selective fire
Feed: Belt
Weight: 18.8kg
Length: 110.5cm
Sights: Blade foresight; leaf rear 300-2,000m; 200m battlesight
Rate of fire: 450 or 700 rounds/min cyclic; 200 rounds/min automatic
Effective range: 1,000m
Manufacturer: Ceskoslovenska Zbrojovka
Status: No longer manufactured. In service in Nigeria and probably elsewhere in Africa.

Model 37 MMG

The MG34 was designed by Mauser-Werke at Oberndorf and was intended as a dual purpose ground and anti-aircraft machine gun. Later it was employed with even greater flexibility and was used as a light machine gun with a bipod and as a sustained-fire machine gun using a sturdy buffered tripod and a dial sight.

The gun was a short recoil design using a rotating bolt head with an interrupted buttress thread at the front. The rear end of the barrel carried two cams which accelerated the bolt rearwards after it was unlocked from the barrel.

The trigger of the standard version produced full automatic fire from the bottom half and single shots from the upper surface. Some, however, were made with a single trigger action producing automatic fire only (see below).

The MG34 remained in service throughout the 1939-45 was and was then taken into service by a number of countries such as Czechoslovakia, France, Israel and, for a time, the East German militia. It has been used by the Viet Cong and North Vietnamese militia, mainly in an anti-aircraft role, and was in use with second-line Portuguese units in Angola. The East German authorities also mounted the MG34 in the SK-1 armoured car which is still believed to be in service.

Ammunition: 7.92mm × 57
Operation: Short recoil, selective fire
Feed: 50-round continuous-link belt or 75-round saddle magazine
Weight: 12kg
Length: 122.5cm; Barrel 63cm
Sights: Blade foresight; leaf notch rear
Rate of fire: 900 rounds/min cyclic; 200 rounds/min automatic
Effective range: 550m from bipod; 1,800 from tripod
Manufacturers: Mauser-Werke; Steyr-Daimler-Puch, (Austria)
Status: No longer in production. In service as indicated in text and possibly elsewhere in Africa or Asia.

MG34

BESA TANK MG   (UNITED KINGDOM)

This was a derivative of the Czech Model 37 MMG (qv) made under licence in the UK by BSA. Originally intended as a tripod-mounted replacement for the Vickers MG it was overtaken by events (in 1939) and was instead adopted as a tank MG, the 7.92mm calibre being retained to save development time.

An unusual feature of the gun is its very short gas cylinder from which, after receiving its initial impulse, the piston is withdrawn completely so that surplus gas and fouling escapes to atmosphere outside the vehicle. As with the Czech weapon the bolt and barrel extensions remain locked during the initial recoil motion and, on the return stroke, the gun fires while the relocked assembly is still moving forwards, thus reducing the recoil force on the mounting.

The BESA was progressively modified through five marks and was phased out with the introduction of the Browning M1919A4 (qv) into British AFV. It has long been withdrawn from UK service but remains in use in countries still using Comet cruiser tanks. A scaled-up version in 15mm calibre was also made but is no longer in service.

Ammunition: 7.92mm × 57
Operation: Gas, automatic
Feed: 225-round metal or metal/fabric belt
Weight: 21.3-24.3kg according to mark
Length: 110.5cm; barrel 73.5cm
Rate of fire: 450 or 750 rounds/min cylic
Effective range: 800m
Manufacturer: Birmingham Small Arms Co.
Status: No longer manufactured. In service (see text) in Burma, Finland, the Irish Republic and South Africa.

0.5in (BROWNING) CALIBRE WEAPONS

Note: Weapons described in this division use the US 0.5inch Browning ammunition which should not be confused with the 12.7mm ammunition used by the weapons described in the next division. The US round has, in all its variants, a smaller charge and a lighter bullet than that of the corresponding Russian 12.7mm × 108 round.

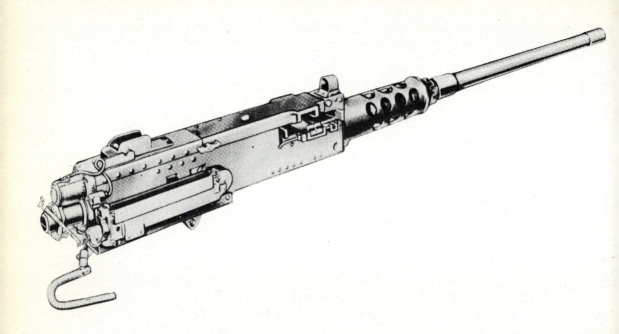

Browning machine guns of .5in calibre originated in a scaled-up version of the .30 M1917 (qv). The development was an urgent response to the realisation, late in 1917, that there was a need for a weapon of greater penetrating power than the .30 gun for effective fire against the protective armour then being used in the European war. The development (which included the development of a suitable round) was a quick one: first firing of a tripod-mounted water-cooled weapon was in October 1918 and an air-cooled aircraft version was fired in the following month.

Progressive improvements led ultimately to three versions of a basic weapon all known by the designation M2 which dates from 1933 although not all versions were in service then. The versions are the basic air-cooled M2, which was used as an aircraft weapon and in some AFV mountings, the M2HB, which was a later air-cooled version with a heavy barrel and could be used in any role, and the M2AA, which was a water-cooled weapon normally fired from the US M3 tripod and used mainly as an anti-aircraft weapon: it may also be encountered, particularly in Asia, mounted on a modified Russian DShK 38/46 mount. The two air-cooled weapons may be easily distinguished by their barrel jackets: the shorter M2 basic weapon has a perforated jacket extending to the muzzle whereas the HB has a length of unjacketed barrel. The gun mechanism is essentially the same as that of the .30 weapon but an oil buffer is incorporated to dissipate the excess recoil energy of the heavier breech block.

One of the most successful guns of all time the .50 Browning is still in widespread service — particularly in AFV mountings. A 4-gun mounting (M-55) on a two-wheel carriage with an armoured shield is still widely used outside the USA and may be encountered also adapted for mounting on US half-track vehicles.

Ammunition: .5 M2 Ball
Operation: Short recoil; automatic fire except M2HB which has selective fire
Feed: Disintegrating link belt
Weight: M2AA 54.9kg (including water) M2HB 38.1kg; M3 Tripod 20kg; M-55 mount complete 975kg
Length: M2AA 167.5cm; M2HB 165.5cm
Sights: Blade foresight, leaf aperture rear. An AA ring sight sometimes fitted
Rate of fire: M2AA 500-650 rounds/min; M2HB 450-550 rounds/min, both cylic
Effective range: 1,000m
Manufacturer: Colt and many others in the USA
Status: No longer in production but still in widespread service in the USA and elsewhere

M2HB Browning MG in turret-mounting configuration

.5in BROWNING AFV MOUNTINGS

Most of the vehicle-mounted .5in Brownings currently in service are to be found in AFV of US manufacture. An important exception is the Netherlands DAF YP-408 APC which mounts an M2HB on the commander's turret, the gun being fired with the hatch covers open. The Japanese SV-60 APC and SX-60 mortar carrier also have M2HB MG mounted, with a simple shield, on the roof and the Type 61 MBT has a M2HB mounted on the commander's hatch. The Austrian Saurer APC has either a M2HB mounted with a shield or a turret-mounted Oerlikon 20mm cannon.

American mountings include AA installations of the M2HB on the Sherman, M24, M41, M47, M48 and M551 tanks, all of which are in service in various parts of the world. Early reconnaissance vehicles include some with open M2HB mountings as also did the original M114. Some M114A1 vehicles and the Lynx command and reconnaissance vehicles made for Canada and the Netherlands however, have an externally-mounted M2HB which can be laid and fired from within the vehicle. The M26 cupola used for these mountings is manually traversed through 360 degrees and the gun manually elevated bet-

Left: *Browning .50MG on DAF YP-408 in service in the Netherlands.*
Above: *This triple mounting comprises two .50 Browning MG and a 37 mm (Browning) gun; it was designed both to increase close-range fire power and to economise on 37 mm ammunition by using*

the .50 guns for sighting. Originally a US weapon system, it is now in service only in Yugoslavia and is probably manufactured there. The system is mounted on a half-track vehicle and had the US designation M15A1

ween −16.5 and +61 degrees. APC mountings are too numerous to list in detail but are mostly open mountings of the M2HB. The M10, M18 and M36 SP ATk guns and the M7, M44, M52, M55, M108 and M109 SP howitzers also carry the weapon.

Far left: The M551 Sheridan tank, in US Army service, has a .50 Browning MG on a roof mounting for use by the commander. The aperture for the 7.62 mm coaxial MG can be seen above and to the right of the driver's head. Left: The commander's .50 Browning MG on the US M48 tank is mounted in a small cupola

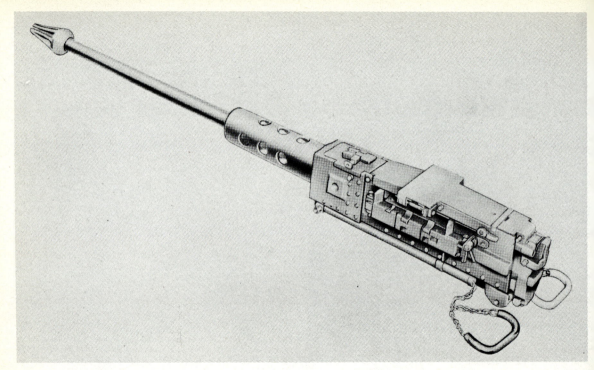

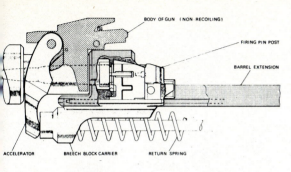

BODY OF GUN (NON-RECOILING)

FIRING PIN POST

BARREL EXTENSION

ACCELERATOR   BREECH BLOCK CARRIER   RETURN SPRING

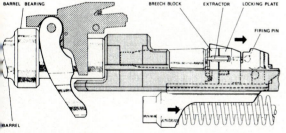

BARREL BEARING   BREECH BLOCK   EXTRACTOR   LOCKING PLATE

FIRING PIN

BARREL

Left: *M85 MG.* Above: *The short recoil action and accelerator of the M85* (RMCS)

This is a recoil-operated weapon designed primarily for coaxial or cupola mounting on AFV but capable of being dismounted and fired from a tripod. Lighter than the M2 Browning, it has a slightly lower muzzle velocity (866 m/sec instead of 893 m/sec with the same ammunition) but has the operational advantage of a choice of rates of fire, the higher of which is about twice that of the Browning.

The gun operates on the short recoil principle, using an accelerator to separate the bolt and barrel after unlocking. The natural cyclic rate is the high one: the lower rate is achieved by holding the working parts to the rear while a delay drum, energised by the recoiling bolt, winds and unwinds under spring control.

Ammunition: .50 M2 Ball
Operation: Short recoil, automatic, with alternative rates of fire
Feed: Disintegrating-link belt
Weight: 27.9kg
Length: 138.5cm; Barrel 91.5cm
Rate of fire: 1,050 rounds/min or 400 rounds/min cyclic
Effective range: 1,000m
Manufacturer: General Electric (USA)
Status: In service with US forces and in many other countries to which the M60 tank has been supplied.

Two mountings for the M85 MG in US AFV have given it a wide distribution. The LVTP-7 amphibious assault vehicle is used by the USMC and in Argentina, Italy, Spain and Thailand, and the M60 series MBT are in service in Austria, Ethiopia, Iran, Israel, Italy, Jordan, Saudi-Arabia, South Korea and Turkey as well as in the US forces. Production of some models of the M60 is continuing but that of the LVTP-7 has ceased.

M60 Series MBT

The M85 is mounted in the commander's cupola of which there are two versions: that in the M60A1 having an M28C sight (which can be changed for an infra-red sight) and eight vision blocks. The cupola can be traversed through 360 degrees and the gun elevated between −15 and +60 degrees. In the M60A2 the commander's turret is fully stabilised, he has a ×8 day periscope and a ×10 night periscope and his cupola has ten vision blocks. The M60A3 version of the tank has various improvements over the M60A1 but none affect the M85 installation.

LVTP-7

The M85 is mounted in the gunner's turret which is provided with vision blocks and ×1 and ×6 sights. Turret traverse is powered and unlimited and the M85 elevation limits are from −15 to +60 degrees. 1,000 rounds of ammunition are carried of which 400 are ready-use.

Manufacturer: M60 — Chrysler Corporation; LVTP-7 — FMC Corporation
Status: In service as indicated above.

US M60A1 MBT with cupola-mounted M85 MG as part of its secondary armament

12.7mm (× 108) CALIBRE WEAPONS

Note. There is only one basic weapon design currently in service in this calibre division — a Russian HMG — but it exists in two versions and a variety of mountings and has been copied for use in the People's Republic of China. Because there are no important differences in either the weapons or the mountings between the Russian and Chinese versions data on the latter are included in the main Russian entry.

QUADRUPLE 12.7mm HEAVY MACHINE GUN MOUNTING M53

This is a mounting designed and built in Czechoslovakia to mount the Soviet DShK 38/46 HMG in a 2 × 2 arrangement similar to that used in the ZPU-4 14.5mm quadruple mounting. It is a two-wheeled mount with levelling jacks at the front and the rear and is recognisable by the four drum magazines used to feed the guns and the prominent muzzle brakes on the barrels. Further information on the basic gun will be found in the appropriate USSR entry.

Calibre: 12.7mm
Dimensions, travelling: 2.9m long × 1.6m wide × 1.78m high

Track: 1.5m
Weight, travelling: 640kg
Weight in combat order: 628kg
Elevator: −7° to +90°
Traverse: 360°
Maximum range: 6,500m horizontal; 5,500m vertical
Effective vertical range: 1,000m
Rate of fire: 550-600 rounds/barrel/min cyclic; Practical 80 rounds/barrel/min
Feed: 50-round drum for each barrel
Status: No longer in service in Czechoslovakia. Believed to be in service in Cuba and Vietnam. Reported to have been installed on BTR-152 APC in Egypt.

114

This is a gas-operated weapon of conventional basic design using a long-stroke piston. Designed by Degtyarev it was based on an earlier model (the DK) of which a few were made in 1934. The feed, however, was designed by Shpagin and was a rotary type in which rounds were removed from the belt links, fed through a feed plate and collected by the bolt as it moved forwards. In this form the weapon was known as the DSh K-38. The feed proved unsatisfactory, however, and weapons made from 1946 onwards, known as the Degtyarev Model 38/46, had a conventional shuttle feed similar to that of the RP-46 Company MG. The Model 38/46 thus has a flat rectangular feed cover which is easily distinguished from the large circular drum mechanism of the earlier version.

Both guns have been used extensively by Warsaw Pact countries and in the Middle East and Far East. The standard ground mounting was a wheeled Sokolov mount (M1938) but it is not now used in Europe although the gun remains in service there in various vehicle mountings. Ground mounts may still be found outside Europe, however, and the gun has been copied in China as the Type 54 HMG. A Czech four-gun AA mounting is described above.

The DSh K-38 feeds from the left only and has a fixed barrel: the M38/46 can be adapted to feed from either side and has a quick-change barrel.

Ammunition: 12.7mm × 108
Operation: Gas, automatic
Feed: 50-round belt
Weight: 35.7kg; Barrel 12.7kg
Length: 159cm; Barrel 107cm
Sights: Cylindrical post foresight; U-notch vertical leaf rear. A M1943 AA sight may be fitted. There is also a coaxial version without sights.
Rate of fire: 575 rounds/min cyclic; 80 rounds/min automatic
Effective range: 2,000m
Status: Probably no longer manufactured. Still in service in Russian and allied armies. Used by Chinese (Type 54), Arab and Vietnamese forces and has been seen with Zimbabwean guerrillas.

Degtyarev HMG

DEGTYAREV HMG VEHICLE MOUNTINGS

With one exception, all current AFV mountings both of the Russian and of the Chinese versions of the Degtyarev HMG are external AA installations. The exception is the T-10 tank, which is still used in Warsaw Pact armies and in Egypt, Syria and Vietnam and which has a coaxial Degtyarev in the main turret as well as on an open AA mounting on the loader's hatch. In the improved T-10M tank these weapons have been replaced by 14.5mm KPVT and KPV HMG.

The other known current installations are:
China: Tanks T-59 (Russian T-54) and T-60 (Russian PT-76); APC K-63.
Czechoslovakia: APC OT-64B (SKOT 2)
USSR: Tanks IS-2, IS-3, T-54, T-62, T-64/72; Reconnaissance Vehicle BRDM-1; Assault Guns ISV-122 and ISV-152.

Left: *DSh K-38 46 on T-55 tank* (Tass). Far left: *T-62A MBT with turret-mounted Degtyarev HMG.* (Tass)

14.5mm CALIBRE WEAPONS

(CZECHOSLOVAKIA / POLAND)

The OT-62C APC is a Polish modification of the Czech OT-62 and is known in Poland as the TOPAS-2AP. It has a turret in which a 14.5mm KPVT HMG and a 7.62mm PKT MG are mounted. In this installation the weapons can be elevated between −5 and +78 degrees and the turret can be traversed through 360 degrees. 500 rounds of 14.5mm and 2,000 rounds of 7.62mm ammunition are carried in the vehicle.

OT-62C AND OT-64C(2) 14.5mm TURRETS

An almost identical and similarly armed turret is installed in the OT-64C(2) APC but the weapon elevation limits for this installation are wider, extending from −4 to +89.5 degrees.

Status: Both vehicles are in service with Polish forces. The OT-64C(1) APC which is more widely used is fitted with a similarly armed turret of Russian design (qv).

(HUNGARY)

The FUG-70 amphibious scout car is equipped with a turret which mounts a 14.5mm KPVT HMG and a 7.62mm PKT MG. The turret is mounted in the centre of the vehicle, is enclosed and has no hatch cover. The 14.5mm gun is mounted in the centre of the turret with the smaller weapon on the left and there is a searchlight, which moves

FUG-70 14.5mm TURRET

with the armament, mounted on the right-hand side of the turret. Elevation limits for the weapons are −5 and +30 degrees, so that only ground targets can be engaged, and the turret can be traversed through 360 degrees.

Status: In service with Hungarian and East German forces.

Left: *The Soviet BTR-60PB APC has a turret similar to that of the OT-64C. The 14.5 mm gun us seen in the foreground of this picture and a second BTR-60PB is in the middle distance* (Tass)

This heavy machine gun works on a short recoil principle with gas assistance supplied by a muzzle booster. After initial recoil and gas assistance the bolt and barrel are unlocked by a cam-operated roller system which also functions as a bolt accelerator. A closed-pocket ammunition belt is used, a round being withdrawn from the belt by feed claws as the bolt recoils and positioned for chambering on the forward stroke.

Designed initially as an anti-aircraft gun it is also suitable for use in AFV, as it has a very short inboard length (60cm), and it is used in the T-10M tank and several other AFV, mainly in the tank configuration known as the KPVT.

There are three towed mountings for the weapon, armed with one two and four HMG and known as ZPU-1, ZPU-2 and ZPU-4 respectively. All are known to exist in China but it is not certain that the weapon has been made there. All these mountings have been very successful and the ZPU-2 and ZPU-4 were used extensively in Vietnam.

Ammunition: 14.5mm
Operation: Short recoil, automatic
Feed: Continuous closed pocket belt
Weight: Gun only 49.1kg; Barrel with jacket 19.5kg
Length: Gun 200.5cm; Barrel 134.5cm
Sights: Cylindrical post foresight; tangent leaf U-notch rear 200-2,000m × 100m
Rate of fire: 600 rounds/min cyclic
Effective range: 2,000m against ground targets. 1,400m AA.
Status: In widespread service in Warsaw Pact and client countries and in China.

Quad-mounted (ZPU-4) KPV HMG on exercises (Tass)

TOWED 14.5mm HMG MOUNTINGS

As noted in the entry for the KPV HMG above, there are three towed mountings for one, two or four of these weapons. Of these the single mount ZPU-1 is believed to be no longer in service in the USSR but has been seen in the Middle East, China and Vietnam. The twin mounting, ZPU-2, is more widely used in Warsaw Pact armies and in the Middle East, China and other parts of Asia; and the quad mounting, ZPU-4, is similarly but possibly less extensively distributed. The mountings have been in service for many years and their presence in China does not necessarily indicate local manufacture.

Brief comparative data are given below.

	ZPU-1	ZPU-2	ZPU-4
Guns	1	2	4
Carriage wheels	2	2	4
Weight Firing	581kg	635kg	2,000kg
Length Travelling	3.9m	3.9m	5.0m
Traverse	360°	360°	360°
Minimum Elevation	−15°	−15°	−10°
Maximum Elevation	+85°	+85°	+90°
Crew	3	4	5

The ZPU-1 and ZPU-2 fire with their wheels raised. The ZPU-4 can fire off its wheels. All have ammunition boxes holding 150 rounds/gun and are equipped with telescopic ground sights and reflex optical AA sights.

Status: As indicated above.

Left: *A close-up of the ZPU-4.* Right: *BTR-152A AA vehicle* (Novosti)

VEHICLE MOUNTINGS FOR 14.5mm HMG

Important current vehicle applications for the KPV/KPVT HMG are described briefly below.

T-10M Tank: As noted in the description of AFV mountings for the 12.7mm Degtyarev MG the modified version of the T-10 tank, known as the T-10M, has 14.5mm KPV and KPVT weapons instead of 12.7mm MG. The KPVT is installed as secondary armament in the main turret and the KPV is an AA mounting on the loader's hatch.

BTR-152A Anti-Aircraft Vehicle: This version of the BTR-152 APC is fitted with a turret mounting twin KPV. The turret and guns are manually traversed and elevated, elevation limits being −5 and +80 degrees. A similar turret is fitted to the BTR-40A anti-aircraft vehicle.

BRDM-2 Reconnaissance Vehicle: The standard model of this vehicle is fitted with a turret armed with a KPVT HMG and a 7.62mm PKT MG. Guns and turret are manually traversed and elevated, elevation limits being −5 and +30 degrees and traverse 360 degrees. The gunner has an integral seat and the weapons are aimed by using a telescope to the left of the KPVT. An infra-red sight can be fitted. There is no hatch cover. 500 rounds of 14.5mm ammunition and 2,000 rounds of 7.62mm ammunition are carried. The same turret is fitted on the BTR-60P APC and the Czech OT-64C(1) APC.

Status: All these mountings are in service, some of them in a great many countries.

20mm CALIBRE WEAPONS

Note. Although all the weapons described in this section are of 20mm calibre, they do not all fire the same ammunition. In view of the relatively small number of different weapons, however, they have been grouped together to avoid a multiplicity of subdivisions and because many of the mountings described here are equally suitable for two or more different weapons. An indication is given of the ammunition appropriate to each weapon.

Range figures are given for some weapons but it should be remembered that such ranges are dependent on the type of ammunition being fired. As a rough guide, however, it may be assumed that a 20mm cannon will have an effective range of around 1,500 metres against an air target and some 2,000 metres against a ground target, maximum lethal range against unprotected targets being three or four times the latter figure.

Sights for these weapons are normally incorporated in the mounting.

Soviet BRDM-2 reconnaissance vehicle (Tass)

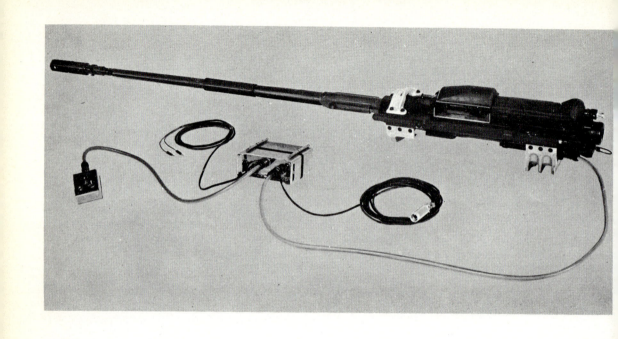

This is a gas-operated cannon of light weight and low recoil designed for use on a small ground vehicle or a cargo carrier.

The gun can fire at single shot from a closed breech or at 300 rounds/minute or 740 rounds/minute. These rates of fire are controlled electrically. In the event of a misfire there is an automatic re-cocking system which uses a blank firing cartridge to provide the necessary power after a delay of 0.3 seconds to allow for a hangfire. It is also possible to re-cock the gun by hand using a wire cable provided with a T handle.

The gun uses mainly the US 20mm M56 cartridge (or the M55 or M53) all of which are electrically fired and allow ready variation of the rate of fire and also permit both open and closed breech firing. These rounds are used in the US M39 20mm Gun and in the Vulcan M61 20mm Gun. The US M12 link is employed.

The feed systems of the gun provide its chief technical interest. The first of the different modes is the usual flat feed with the belt coming in from one side and the empty links ejected on the opposite side. The direction of feed can be reversed by the reversal of the sprocket feed and by changing several parts. The second method is referred to as the "enveloping feed mechanism". It uses the same

arrangements except that the axis of the sprocket drive has been raised so that the rounds enter the gun from a slightly elevated position and the links are ejected on the same side as the feed and are flung out under the incoming belt. The third system is a flat feed system but a generator is built into the gun and no external power is required. Lastly, there is a double feed with two belts, one on each side. The gunner is able to select which of the two belts he requires and so can change from HE to AP at will. With all four methods of feed, the electrical control box enables the firer to select single shot fire with a closed breech operation, or automatic fire from an open breech. At automatic the length of the burst can be fixed and a record maintained of the rounds fired.

Ammunition: 20mm calibre. See text
Operation: Gas, electrically controlled
Feed: Belt. See text
Weight: Gun 45.5kg; Cradle 12.5kg
Length: 220.5cm
Width: 20cm in cradle
Height: Gun in cradle 24.5cm; 42.5cm with selective feed
Rate of fire: 700 or 300 rounds/min
Power supply: 24V where required (see text)
Supplier: GIAT
Status: In production and in service with French and other forces.

M621 cannon

The F2 is a gas operated cannon with two gas vents, one on each side of the barrel, and a short gas piston in each of the cylinders which is driven back as the gas passes through the vents. The gun is locked by two swinging locking pieces which are used in the locked position as struts between the block and the body of the gun. The gas pressure, after firing, drives back the two pistons and they in turn move back the supports which hold the locking pieces in place, and the residual gas pressure forces the breech block rearwards.

The gun fires cartridges with the mechanical primer of the Hispano Suiza HS820 family — as opposed to the M621 which uses the electrically primed USA M56 cartridge. The feed system allows the choice of two types of ammunition. These are held in belts fed in from each side and rapid change from one to the other is possible using a manually operated switch. The feed on each side is known to the manufacturer as "enveloping" and this entails the ejection of the links from the same side as the belt feed. The feed mechanism is driven mechanically by the recoiling movement of the breech block slides, through a ratchet and pawl assembly. The weapon when used with a power source can be remotely controlled. The control box allows the selection of single shot, automatic fire or a limited burst.

Ammunition: 20mm (see text)
Operation: Gas, selective fire, optional remote operation
Feed: Dual-feed belt
Weight: 80kg; Barrel 25kg; Cradle 10.5kg
Length: 260cm
Width: 20.5cm
Height: 26cm
Rate of fire: 700-780 rounds/min
Supplier: GIAT
Status: Production and service

20 mm F2 (M693) cannon

TARASQUE LIGHT TOWED AA MOUNTING TYPE 53 T2

This is a one-man operated unit which can be towed by any vehicle and is designed for use with the F2 cannon. Important features are optional manual or hydraulic laying and a quick-replacement box for the HE ammunition. An hydraulic recocking device is fitted.

Weight: 660kg firing; 840kg with trailer
Traverse: unlimited; 10° per handle revolution
Elevation: −8° to +83°; 6.5° per handle revolution
Hydraulic laying: 0-40°/sec in traverse; 0-80°/sec in elevation
Sights: × 1 for AA targets; × 5.2 for ground targets
Ammunition carried: 100 HE and 40 AP
Crew: 1
Supplier: GIAT (made by EFAB)
Status: Production

Tarasque (53 T2) mounting

130

TRUCK MOUNTING 15A FOR M621 GUN

This light mounting is designed for installation on an open vehicle with the gunner standing behind the mount. A radio link is provided to enable the gunner to communicate with the cab. The mounting can also be used on naval or riverine craft. The gun is installed with a left-hand enveloping feed.

Weight: 225kg including 160 rounds
Traverse: 360° in either direction
Elevation: −10° to +45°
Sight: Collimator with night firing illumination
Ammunition carried: 160 rounds
Crew: 1
Supplier: GIAT (made by EFAB and MAT)
Status: Production

Truck-mounted M621 cannon

CERBERE TWIN TOWED AA MOUNTING

This is a relatively elaborate twin mounting for F2 cannon. It features a computer sight (P56) and joystick-controlled fast power elevation and traverse. Hydraulic recocking is provided for the guns. Power for the hydraulic gun-laying is supplied by an hydraulic pump-engine, but the guns can also be laid manually. The whole is mounted on a two-wheel trailer. Apart from the guns the mounting is substantially the same as the Rheinmetall Rh202 twin mounting (qv).

Weight: 2,100kg all up
Traverse: Unlimited; 10° per handwheel revolution
Elevation: −5° to +83°; 4.5° per handwheel revolution
Hydraulic laying: 0-80°/sec in traverse; 0-50°/sec in elevation
Sight: Computer sight calculates lead angles with optical sight on target
Optics: × 5 magnification; 12° field
Ammunition supply: 570 rounds HS 820 in two boxes
Supplier: GIAT (made by EFAB)

Cerbère twin towed AA mounting

CENTAURE TWIN TOWED MOUNTING

This is a rugged and relatively simple mounting for two F2 cannon. It is manually operated and optically laid and can be used to engage either ground or aircraft targets. Two traverse speeds are available. The mounting platform has two wheels which are folded up for firing.

Weight: 914kg all up except ammunition
Traverse: Unlimited: 28.5° or 9.8° per handwheel revolution
Elevation: −5° to +85°; 8.5° per revolution
Sights: × 1 with correction curves for AA; × 4 for ground targets
Ammunition supply: 200 HS 820 rounds in two boxes
Supplier: GIAT (made by EFAB)

Centaure twin towed mounting

CB 20 LIGHT VEHICLE MOUNTING

This is a simple open roof mounting for a 20mm cannon (M621 HS820 or M151) and comprises a base ring, for attachment to the vehicle, on which rotates a gun, shield and ammunition box assembly. Electric power for firing the gun is supplied through a slip-ring. Laying is manual and sighting optical. When not in use the hatch can be sealed by semicircular covers. A searchlight can be fitted.

Weight: 200kg without gun; approximately 390kg with gun
Traverse: Unlimited
Elevation: −5° to +65°
Sight: × 3 magnification
Ammunition supply: 75 rounds in box
Manufacturer: Creusot-Loire
Status: Development.

Far left: *20 mm cannon on a CB.20 mounting on a Panhard 6x6 ERC.*
Left: *CB.20 light vehicle mounting*

TOUCAN I VEHICLE MOUNTING

This is an external mounting for a 20mm cannon (French M621 with single feed, F2 with dual feed or German Rh202) which can be laid and fired from within the vehicle. The gun, together with its ammunition, an optional searchlight and smoke dischargers and — again optionally — a 7.62mm coaxial MG, is mounted on a small cupola which is available in light and heavy versions according to the degree of armour protection required. The system is operated by one man who is provided with a × 6 day sight with a frontal episcope for ground fire, a collimator sight for AA fire, an external sight for direct aiming, six episcopes for lateral vision and a variety of optional facilities. Provision is made for restricting fire in predetermined zones according to the nature of the installation.

Weight: About 540-730kg according to armour and armament

Traverse: 360° or more according to installation type; Rate 12°/sec

Elevation: $-13°$ to $+50°$; Rate 16°/sec

Sights: See text

Ammunition supply: One or two boxes according to weapon used. 96 rounds for single input or 45AP and 75HE for double input

Supplier: GIAT (made by MAS)

Status: Production. Exported to several countries on French armoured vehicles.

Left: *Typical arrangement of Toucan I mounting.* Above: *Toucan on a 6x6 VAB*

TOUCAN II VEHICLE MOUNTING

This two-man turret mounting is used on the AMX-10PH APC and in that configuration it is armed with a 20mm F2 cannon and a .30 (Browning) coaxial MG. It can, however, be used with the M621 or German Rh202 cannon and any of several MG. Smoke projectors can also be fitted.

The turret is designed to be operated by the vehicle commander and a gunner, both of whom can aim and fire the weapons with automatic priority to the commander. Both have × 6 sights with frontal episcopes and the commander also has a collimator sight for AA fire and access to an open sight with the turret flaps open. If required the gunner's sight may be replaced by a day/night sight. A long-range searchlight is fitted and there are seven episcopes for all-round vision with the flaps closed. The turret

provides NBC protection and there is a transparent cupola to protect the commander when the flaps are open. Provision is made for restricting fire in predetermined zones.

Weight: 1,312kg in combat order on AMX-10PH
Traverse: 360° or more according to installation type; Rates 10°/sec manual or up to 50°/sec automatic
Elevation: −8° to +50°; Rates 26°/sec manual or up to 30°/sec automatic
Sights: See text
Ammunition supply: 260 rounds HE and 65 AP (on AMX-10PH) and 200 rounds MG in replaceable box
Supplier: GIAT (made by MAS)
Status: In production and in service with the French Army.

Toucan II mounting. Note the feed for the 7.62 mm MG

SAMM SINGLE-GUN TURRETS

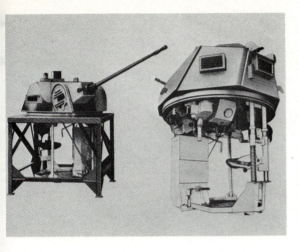

SAMM (Société d'Applications des Machines Motrices) make a range of one-man and two-man turrets for one or two 20mm cannon and various other weapons. There are three basic types of single-gun turret.

S 20 Light Turret: This is operated by one man and is fitted with an episcope sight type M 411 giving × 6 viewing with a 10 degree field for ground targets and × 1 viewing for air targets with a field of 77 degrees in azimuth and 32 in elevation and a collimator field of 14 degrees. Four armoured viewing blocks provide supplementary viewing without blind arcs. The turret is normally fitted with an F2 cannon, but a variant (TF 20) exists with a German Rh202 and the turret can be adapted to take the HSS 820. Normal laying is manual but it can be powered.

TG 120 Scout Turret: This in its standard form is a two-man turret suitable for installation on reconnaissance and similar vehicles. Each man has a type M411 dual-purpose sight (see above) and six episcopes are provided to complete the all-round view. Standard armament is a F2 cannon, a 7.62mm (or 7.5mm) coaxial MG and four smoke dischargers, and a multiple grenade-launcher can be mounted on the roof and fired from within the turret. The TG120 has powered laying and provides NBC protection. Two variants are available: one is a one-man simplified turret with the commander's sight replaced by an episcope and options of removing the MG, reducing the NBC protection, converting the turret to an open type and so forth: the

Left: *The TSR-3S stabilised turret.* Above: *Two views of the S.20 turret*

other is a more elaborate version fitted with the Rapace battlefield radar or a TV viewing system and other additional facilities.

TSR 3S Stabilised Turret: This is a two-man turret designed for use with infantry combat vehicles and providing a capability for accurate fire on the move across rough country. Vehicle roll and pitch is compensated up to 12 degrees either side of the horizontal and heading changes are fully compensated. The specification calls for 70 per cent direct hits on a four square metre target at 800-1,000 metres with the vehicle weaving at 30km/h over rough terrain. The turret is armed with a 20mm F2 or Rh202 cannon and a 7.62mm (or 7.5mm) MG and six smoke pots. Both commander and gunner have M411 sights (see above) and both can aim and fire the weapons with automatic priority to the commander. Six M223 episcopes are provided for all-round vision. The weapons are power-laid. The designation TSR 3S applies to the version with the F2 cannon: that with the Rh202 is designated LWT-3 and for this turret the MG is the MG3A1.

	S20	TG120	TSR3S
Crew:	1	2	2
Combat weight:	750kg	1,700kg	2,200kg
Max depression:	−8°	−8°	−13°
Max elevation:	+60°	+50°	+77°
Max laying rate:	9°/sec	50°/sec	70°/sec
Armour:	6mm	12-15mm	15-20mm

Manufacturer: SAMM

Status: S20 prototype; TF20 production; TG120 evaluation; TSR 3S development; LWT-3 prototype

SAMM S 530 SERIES TWIN-GUN MOUNTINGS

S530 twin-gun turret on a Panhard AML

Primarily designed for AA operation, the SAMM twin-gun mountings for 20mm weapons can also be used to engage ground targets. They are manned by two men. There are two groups of mountings; the S 530 series mount the guns at the front of the turret while the Sabre series have the gun mounts at the rear and on either side of the turret.

The S530A is a light and simple mounting for small AFV and is armed with two M621 cannon. These are aimed and fired by the gunner who has an M411 sight (see previous entry). Gunlaying is hydraulic, with an emergency manual option, power being supplied by an electric pump. Seven episcopes (four for the commander and three for the gunner) provide all-round vision. A small version of the S530A is known as S531, and there are open-top, S532, and HSS 820, S533, versions.

Weight: about 1,700kg (S530A)
Traverse: Unlimited; 80°/sec
Elevation: −10° to +70°; 50°/sec
Ammunition supply: 260 rounds/gun in turret basket
Manufacturer: SAMM
Status: In production and in service in one country outside France.

SAMM SABRE TURRETS

This series of two-man turrets has a common basic design which is suitable for mounting a diversity of pairs of weapons and for the addition of radar or other facilities. The weapons are mounted on the sides of the turret at the rear, thus making it easy to provide a good view from the cupola top of the turret.

Two turret patterns are specified for 20mm cannon mountings on land vehicles, Sabre-15 and Sabre-18, the latter being the larger. Both can mount F2 or HSS 820 cannon and the Sabre-18 can mount the Rh202. A coaxial 7.62mm MG can be added to one of the cannon mountings. Each man is provided with an M411 dual-purpose sight (see previous entries) and all-round vision is provided by episcopes. Laying is hydraulic with power supplied by an electric pump and there is an option of servo control. Emergency manual control is provided. Turrets can be adapted for mounting on naval vessels.

	Sabre-15	Sabre-18
Weight:	about 1,600kg	about 2,000kg
Max Depression:	$-10°$	$-10°$
Max elevation:	$+80°$	$+85°$
Max slewing speed:	90°/sec	90°/sec
Armour:	8-12mm	10-15mm
Ammunition supply:	500 HE	520 HE
	30 AP	30 AP

Manufacturer: SAMM

Status: Sabre-15 is in development: Sabre-18 prototypes had been test-fired before mid-1977. A version equipped with radar, fire-control computer and more elaborate optics has been specified for the VADAR SP AA weapon system which is being developed under GIAT auspices for the French Army.

Twin-gun turret for the VADAR SP AA system

This turret has been designed for use on internal security and similar light vehicles. Its primary armament mounted on an armature at the front of the turret is a 60mm mortar (60 CS DTAT or Brandt HB 60) and its secondary armament can be one or two MG or a 20mm cannon. Operated by two men it is equipped with a M112/3 sight for use against ground targets and seven episcopes. A searchlight is coupled to the armament and another can be mounted on the roof as also can an external MG. The weapons are laid manually.

Weight: about 1,200kg all up
Traverse: Unlimited
Elevation: −8° to +60° (+80° for the mortar)
Ammunition Supply: 500 rounds 20mm and 30-50 mortar rounds according to type and role.
Manufacturer: CNMP
Status: In production and in widespread service.

This mounting for twin HS 820 cannon is the basis of the TA20 light mobile AA weapon system developed by EMD. The turret is operated by one man and is equipped with an EMD surveillance and target designation radar, an Officine Galileo computer sight and six episcopes for all-round vision. A coaxial 7.62mm MG (AA 52 NF-1), with 200 ready rounds, is mounted on one cannon and a searchlight on the other for use against ground targets. Gunlaying is hydraulic with emergency manual drives.

Weight: about 1,900kg all-up
Traverse: Unlimited; Rate 90°/sec
Elevation: −5.5° to +85°; Rate 80°/sec
Sight: Galileo P56T × 5 with 12° field
Ammunition Supply: 325 rounds/gun 20mm. 200 rounds 7.62mm
Manufacturers: TA 20 System, Electronique Marcel Dassault
H20R Turret, CNMP
Status: Series Production.

The TA20 light mobile AA weapon system

The Hotchkiss SP 1A reconnaissance vehicle, known in Germany — where it is in service — as the SPZ 11-2 Halbgruppe Kurz, has a turret-mounted HS 820 20mm cannon. The turret is equipped with a periscope with magnifications of × 4 and × 15 and can be traversed through 360 degrees. The gun elevation limits are −20 to +75 degrees. 500 rounds of 20mm ammunition are carried.

Vehicle Manufacturer: Hotchkiss-Brandt
Status: In service in Germany.

SERVAL 60/20 MOUNTING

This is a versatile turret designed for installation on light AFV. Its armament comprises a 60mm mortar (60 CS DTAT, HB 60 or HB60LR) mounted on an armature at the front and a 20mm cannon (M621, F2 or HS 820 SL) mounted at the rear. A 7.62mm MG can be mounted externally. Operated by two men the turret is equipped with a sighting periscope and nine viewing episcopes and various optional aids. The weapons are laid manually. NBC protection is optional.

Weight: 1,400-1,700kg according to armament
Traverse: Unlimited
Elevation: about −8° to +50° (+80° for mortar)
Ammunition Supply: 250-325 20mm rounds according to type. About 50 mortar bombs
Manufacturer: CNMP
Status: Prototype vehicle installations include the Panhard 4 × 4 AML-60-20 and 6 × 6 ERC-60-20.

Panhard AML with Serval 60/20 mounting

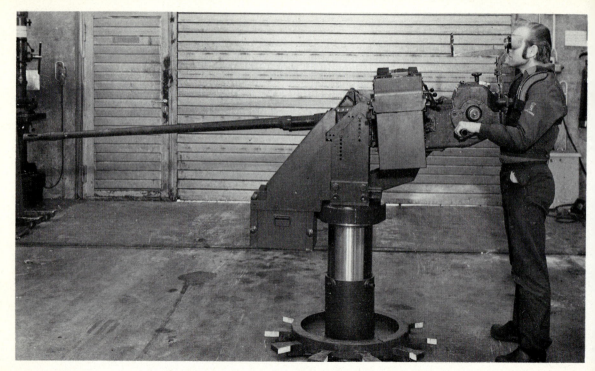

Designed for use against aircraft or ground targets, the Rh202 is gas-operated and fires while the working parts are moving forward so that a large part of the recoil energy is taken to arrest and then reverse this motion. This "floating" firing and the use of a muzzle brake keep the recoil force down to 550-700kg.

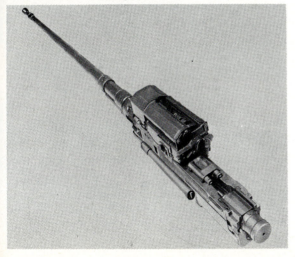

The low recoil force and the use of gas pressure instead of recoil to operate the feed lead to a low trunnion pull, so that the gun can be installed in a very light mounting on a vehicle which normally would be overstressed with a 20mm gun of conventional recoil force. The gun has two different belt fed systems. Each is mounted on a hinged frame which is separate from the gun and absorbs the forces involved in the passage of the ammunition. The Type 2 belt feed mechanism allows two belts to be fed in together, side by side, into the top of the gun. These belt feeds originate one on each side of the weapon and allow a very rapid change from one type of ammunition to the other, merely by throwing over a switch on the feed mechanism.

The Type 3 belt feed mechanism allows the feed of two belts one from each side and at the same time a magazine can be inserted from the top. It is possible with this feed to fire alternate rounds from two belts in turn. This can be done manually or an external source of electric or hydraulic power can be used.

Numerous mountings have been devised for the Rh202, the more important of which for land forces are described in later entries. Naval mountings are also available.

Far left: Single Rh 202 on a KV naval mounting (pre-prototype).
Left: Rh 202 cannon

Ammunition: 20mm × 139
Operation: Gas; selective fire
Feed: Belts or belts plus magazine (see text)
Weight: 81.5kg; Barrel 28kg
Length: 261cm
Width: Gun 11cm; 24cm with Type 2 feed
Height: 26cm
Rate of fire: 800-1,000 rounds/min cyclic
Effective range: 2,000 metres (ground targets); Maximum 7,000 metres
Manufacturer: Rheinmetall
Status: In production and in service in West Germany, Italy and Norway at least.

RHEINMETALL AA TWIN MOUNTING

This is a power-laid mounting (with emergency manual operation) for two Rh202 cannon. Designed primarily for AA operations it can also be used to engage ground targets. An Officine Galileo P56 computer sight is provided for fire control and this incorporates a 'taboo' facility which prevents the gun from being fired in prohibited directions — thus avoiding the commonly encountered danger of firing on friendly troops when operating any kind of aided laying system. The arrangement permits the specification of an elaborate series of prohibited azimuth and elevation combinations.

To engage an air target the gunner first sets estimated target speed and aiming point distance on the input panel then acquires the target in his open sight using the joystick to control the gun. He then changes over to the optical sight and uses the joystick to bring the reticle into coincidence with the nose of the aircraft. Holding the sight in this relative position by means of the joystick he then presses the joystick down to put the guns under control of the computer. Thereafter he keeps the optical sight on the target and the computer points the guns with the degree of lead needed for successful firing. Firing will, however, be inhibited when appropriate by the taboo programme.

Extreme left: *Single Rh202 mounting on a Kraka truck.* Centre left: *S20/2 single naval mounting for the Rh 202.* Left: *AA twin mounting in firing position*

When engaging ground targets it is necessary only to set the estimated range on the input panel and to bring the target into the reticle of the optical sight before firing.

The mounting is towed on a two-wheel trailer, the wheels being detached when the mounting is deployed. System power is supplied by a built-in petrol-electric generator.

Weight: 2,170kg travelling, without ammunition. 1,640kg firing with 550 rounds
Traverse: Unlimited. Rate 80°/sec
Elevation: −7.5° to +85.5°. Rate 48°/sec
Sight: Galileo P56 with × 5 magnification and 12° field
Ammunition supply: 2 boxes of 275 belted rounds each
Manufacturer: Rheinmetall
Status: In production and in service with German and other NATO forces.

Rheinmetall Rh 202 AA twin mount on tow

HS 820 ON SPZ 12-3 APC

The SPZ 12-3 APC is equipped with a turret-mounted HS820 20mm cannon made in Germany by Rheinmetall. The gun is power laid, the turret having 360 degrees traverse and the elevation limits being from −10 degrees to +75 degrees.

Vehicle Manufacturer: Henschel and Hanomag. Also made in UK by Leyland.
Status: In German Army service. Production complete.

Designed by Keller and Knappich of Augsburg, the Rh202 installation on the Marder MICV is a two-man turret with powered gunlaying (with emergency manual laying). Both commander and gunner are equipped with Periz 11 periscopes with magnifications of × 2 and × 6 and these can be changed to infra-red sights for night firing. An infra-red/white searchlight is mounted on the turret. Eleven observation periscopes are provided, eight for the commander and three for the gunner. A 7.62mm MG3 MG is mounted coaxially with the cannon and there are six smoke dischargers on the front of the turret. The Rh202 has a Type 3 feed system giving a choice of three types of ammunition.

Weight: 2,300kg all up
Traverse: Unlimited; Rate 60°/second
Elevation: −17° to +65°; Rate 40°/second
Ammunition supply: 345 rounds 20mm and 500 rounds 7.62mm in turret
Vehicle manufacturer: Rheinstahl, Kassel
Status: In service in the German Army

Rh 202 installation on Marder MICV

Rh202 ON RADSPAHPANZER 2

Main armament of the Radspähpanzer 2 reconnaissance vehicle is a turret-mounted Rh202 cannon. The turret is power operated and has a high slewing speed through 360 degrees. Gun elevation limits are −15 degrees to +55 degrees and an infra-red/white searchlight is elevated by the gun armature. When closed the turret provides NBC protection.

Vehicle manufacturer: Rheinstahl, Kassel
Status: In production and in service with the German Army

RHEINMETALL TF 20.15 TURRET

This is another Rheinmetall one-man turret for the Rh 202 cannon. It is manually operated and its small size and low weight make it suitable for installation on either wheeled or tracked light AFV. The Rh202 is internally mounted and the weapon and fighting compartments are separated by a gastight bulkhead. The operator has an × 4 sighting periscope, for ground and air targets, two observation periscopes and four vision blocks.

Weight: 612kg with ammunition but unmanned
Traverse: Unlimited; Rate (manual) 9.3°/sec max
Elevation: −6° to +60°; Rate (manual) 6·5°/sec
Sights: × 4 periscope with 15° field
Ammunition supply: 220 rounds 20mm
Options: Coaxial MG, smoke dischargers, searchlight, night vision equipment etc
Manufacturer: Rheinmetall

Rheinmetall TF 20.15 one-man turret

Rh202 ON 6616M ARMOURED CAR

The Type 6616M armoured car jointly developed by Fiat and Oto Melara is armed, in its standard version, with a 20mm Rh202 cannon, a coaxial 7.62mm MG, a 40mm grenade launcher, a smoke grenade launcher and two smoke dischargers, all mounted on a turret. Gunlaying is fully powered with emergency manual laying facilities. The commander has the grenade launcher mounted on the roof of his hatch and can load and fire it from within the vehicle and he has nine periscopes for all-round viewing. The gunner has a combined sight and observation periscope.

Traverse: 360°; Rate 40°/sec
Elevation: −5° to +35°; Rate 25°/sec
Ammunition supply: 250 rounds 20mm and 300 rounds 7.62mm in turret
Vehicle Manufacturer: Fiat, Turin, and Oto Melara, La Spezia
Status: Production.

Far right: *HS 669 N towed mounting for Rh 202.* Right: *Fiat/OTO Melara 661M armoured car with Rh 202 cannon*

AA FIELD MOUNTING HS 669 N

This towed mounting for the Rh202 cannon was a cooperative development by Rheinmetall and Kern in Germany, Hispano Suiza (now Oerlikon) in Switzerland and Kongsberg in Norway as project leader. The mounting may be used to engage both air and ground targets, is simple and easy to operate and may be brought into action quickly. Normally towed on a two-wheel trailer it may also be transported by aircraft or helicopter and can be broken down into man-pack loads.

The mounting is a development of the HS669 Hispano-Suiza mounting (now designated Oerlikon GAI-C) adapted for use with the Rh202 weapon with Type 3 feed (qv). Twin ammunition boxes on either side of the gun hold 75 rounds each and a 10-round magazine is inserted in the top of the gun. The Kern FERO-Z13 sight is used for both ground and air targets. Lead angle curves are provided to assist with the engagement of air targets and for ground targets the sight is calibrated for ranges of 500, 1,000 and 1,500 metres.

Gunlaying is manual by handwheels and the gunner's seat, which is designed for use in the AA role, can be folded to provide him with a comfortable support in the prone position for ground fire.

Weight: 620kg total; Carriage 160kg
Sight: × 5 ground and × 1.5 air
Manufacturer: A/S Kongsberg Våpenfabrikk (see text)

MEROKA AA SYSTEM

CETME have for some years been working on multi-barrel gun systems for AA defence on land or at sea. Little information has so far been made available, but it appears that several types of mounting with weapons of several different calibres have been taken to experimental stages and that at least one ground version has been taken to the prototype stage and its naval counterpart ordered for service. This is a 12-barrel weapon of 20mm calibre which is designated Meroka 12-203. Similar configurations in 25mm and 30mm calibre have been designated Meroka 12-253 and 12-303 respectively and it is believed that there are designations Meroka 8-353 (35mm, eight barrels) and 6-403 (40mm, six barrels).

It appears that the weapon assemblies comprise arrays of cannon, operating on principles similar to those of the Oerlikon KAB series (qv) but firing special ammunition in salvoes. Reported shell weights are not markedly different from those for more conventional weapons and it would appear that the primary purpose of the technique is to obtain a scatter-gun effect, filling the airspace with high velocity projectiles.

The naval installation of the 12-203 has its 120-calibre barrels arranged in two rows of six. It has an optical gyro sight for target acquisition after which it functions automatically under radar control. It is being installed on several Spanish ships and all installations were scheduled to be operational by late 1977. No operational date is known for the land force system.

HS TYPE 804 ON PBV 302 APC

A turret mounting for the Hispano-Suiza Type 804 cannon (now no longer in the Oerlikon range) is installed on the Swedish Pbv 302 APC. This gun has a cyclic rate of fire of 500 rounds/min and a muzzle velocity of 800m/sec with AP rounds — both figures being substantially lower than those of current Oerlikon types. Gun laying is manual and the gunner is provided with a × 8 monocular sight for ground targets and uses open sights (with the hatch cover open) for AA fire; he also has three forward-looking periscopes and a fourth in the rear of the turret. Firing torque is automatically compensated.

Traverse: 360°: Gearing selectable from 4° to 12° per handle revolution
Elevation: −10° to +50°
Ammunition Supply: Three belts of 135 rounds HE and 10 10-round AP magazines
Vehicle Manufacturer: AB Hägglund and Söner
Status: Production complete. Vehicle in service.

HS 804 cannon on Pbv 302 APC

This weapon is the latest in a series of improvements on a basic design dating from before the Second World War. It is a light AA weapon used by brigade AA units in the Swedish Army. Mounted on a two-wheel trailer for towing it is supported on a three-part trail with the wheels raised when firing.

Ammunition: 20mm
Weight: 500kg in combat order
Barrel: 70 calibre
Traverse: 360°
Elevation: −5° to +35°
Rate of fire: 360 rounds/min
Status: In service in Sweden.

The Brazilian Urutu APC has the same cannon mounting as the Pbv 302 APC

OERLIKON TYPE KAD (FORMERLY HS 820)

The Hispano-Suiza designed HS 820 has been one of the most successful 20mm guns ever produced. It has been used in a number of mounts for a variety of tasks by the armed forces of many nations including the USA and Germany, and the same mechanism has been adopted for a 30mm gun, the HS 831. The current Oerlikon equivalents are the KAD-AO1, which can have either drum or box magazine feed, and KAD-B which is the general designation of a family of belt-fed weapons. Of this family the KAD-B13-3 and KAD-B17 have right-hand feed and the KAD-B16 left-hand feed; and the B13-3 has an axially-mounted recoil buffer whereas the other two have offset buffers.

The gun is gas-operated, gas tapped from the barrel being used to unlock the breech after initial recoil and residual pressure separating the bolt from the breech to perform the feed cycle. The gun fires from the open breech position.

Ammunition: 20mm
Operation: Blowback with locked breech. Selective fire
Feed: 10-round box, 50 round drum (KAD-AO1) or belt (KAD-B)
Weight: Gun only 61kg (AO1) or 57kg (B). With feed but no ammunition 63 or 65.8kg (AO1) or 65.5kg (B). Barrels 35kg and 31kg
Length: 297.5cm or 256.5cm. Barrels 231.5cm (105 calibres) or 190.5cm (85 calibres)
Rate of fire: 1,000 rounds/min max
Manufacturer: Machine Tool Works Oerlikon Bührle
Status: KAD models in production and service. HS 820 no longer made in Switzerland but still in widespread use. The US licence-built version is known as the M 139 and is in service with US forces.

Oerlikon 20 mm KAD cannon

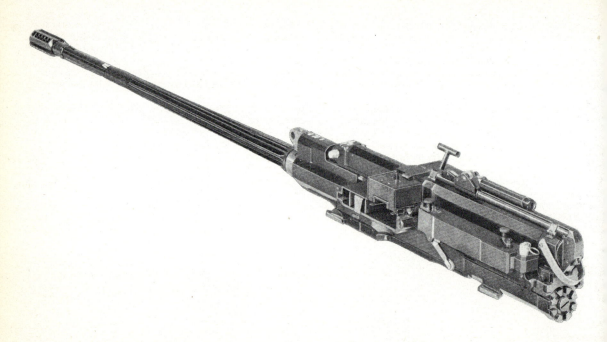

OERLIKON TYPE KAA (FORMERLY 204GK)

Like the HS 820 (Oerlikon KAD) this is a blowback-operated gun with a gas-operated breech unlocking mechanism. It fires from the open breech position and when operating cyclically the round is fired during the barrel recuperation period, thus giving 'floating firing'. Versions with light and heavy barrels are made.

The gun is belt-fed and the feed mechanism is operated by the return spring housing. A lug on this engages in a spiral slot in the feed cylinder and the cylinder rotates first in one direction and then in the other. At the front end of the cylinder, teeth are cut which engage in the feed slide and move it across the gun and back. As it moves in, the feed pawls attached to it bring the next round in front of the bolt. The belt is prevented from slipping back by the stop pawl as the feed slide moves out to collect the next round.

Ammunition: 20mm
Operation: Blowback with locked breech. Selective fire
Feed: Disintegrating-link belt
Weight: 87kg. Barrel 26.6kg. Add 5.7kg for heavy barrel
Barrel length: 85 calibres
Rate of fire: 1,000 rounds/min cyclic
Manufacturer: Machine Tool Works Oerlikon Bührle
Status: In production and in service

Oerlikon type KAA

This is a positively-locked gas-operated gun suitable for AA or ground target applications. It is mechanically fired and uses a mechanical trigger, for either single-shot or automatic operation, with a trigger locking device which prevents the bolt from moving forward without feeding a round into the chamber. Ammunition feed is by either drum or box magazine. The barrel has Oerlikon progressive rifling and is fitted with a 4-stage muzzle brake.

The GAI-BO1 mounting (formerly 101La/5TG) is a towed two-wheel trailer which can be used to engage ground targets while on its wheels or either ground or air targets with its frame on the ground. It has good cross-country performance and with ground clearance adjustable from 23cm to 37cm it can traverse most terrain.

Ammunition: 20mm
Operation: Blowback with locked breech. Selective fire
Feed: 8-round box-magazine or 20-round or 50-round drum
Weight: 109kg excluding magazine. Barrel 51.6kg. Add approx 7.8, 23.6 or 41kg for loaded magazine
Barrel length: 240cm
Rate of fire: approx 1,000 rounds/min
Traverse: Unlimited 3 seconds for 360°
Elevation: −50° to +85° in 2 seconds
Time into action: 20-25 seconds
Manufacturer: Machine Tool Works Oerlikon Bührle, Zurich
Status: In production and in service. The KAB-001 gun is also to be found in a coaxial mounting as secondary turret armament of the Swiss Pz61 main battle tank.

Oerlikon type KAB

The Oerlikon 20mm cannon KAD formerly known by its Hispano-Suiza designation, HS 820, has been used in many different mountings, some of which are described below.

GAI-C Single Mounting

Formerly designated HS 669A, this is a mobile single gun mounting from which three men can get the gun into action against aircraft in 20 seconds and get out again after action in a further 20 seconds. The weight of the complete equipment in the travelling position is 512kg and in the firing position 370kg. The length in the travelling position is 4.04 metres and when in the firing position the width is 1.70 metres and the distance from the pivot to muzzle 2.65 metres. The mounting has since been superseded by the GAI-CO1 and GAI-CO3 single mountings.

HS 665 Triple Mounting

This was a mobile mounting with self-contained fire and power control equipment for three type HS 820 guns, enabling them to be used in the anti-aircraft and anti-armour roles as well as against soft targets. There is a two wheel carriage which can easily be withdrawn when the equipment is brought into action by its detachment (including the driver) of four. Only a gunner and a loader are needed to maintain fire. On the ground the gun is supported on three spades to form a wide and rigid base. The gunner controls the fire from the back of the mounting and uses a joystick assembly. There are two prismatic sights fitted — one for anti-aircraft use and one for ground targets. Hydraulic power is used to elevate and traverse the gun, the system having been devised by Officine Galileo of Florence.

Weight: 1,570kg travelling; 1,230kg firing
Traverse: 360° Rate 110°/sec
Elevation: −3° to +81° mechanical; −5° to +83° hydraulic Rate 60°/sec (hydraulic)

Single Mountings GAI-CO1 and GAI-CO3

Successors to the GAI-C mounting, these two light single mountings differ in only two significant respects: the GAI-CO1 is belt-fed and incorporates the KAD-B13-3 85 calibre cannon whereas the GAI-CO3 is drum-fed and has the longer-barrelled 105 calibre KAD-AO1 cannon.

Both are one-man operated and tripod-mounted, with detachable two-wheel travelling gear which has an adjustable towing eye. They have reflector sights for use against air and ground targets with a fixed arrangement of lead markers and lead curves which automatically follow the elevation movements of the gun.

Single mounting type GAI-CO1

173

Weight, travelling: 512kg (CO1); 495kg (CO3)
Weight, firing: 370kg (CO1); 342kg (CO3)
Traverse: Unlimited (free movement or foot pedal)
Elevation: −7° to +83°; 8° per handwheel revolution
Sights: Delta IV reflector sight for AA and telescopic (× 2.5) sight for ground targets

GAI-DO1 Twin Mounting (HSS 666)

This is a Hispano Oerlikon twin barrel mounting using the HS 820 (KAD) cannon for low level air defence. The gun mounting has hydraulic power control using the Galileo control unit P56 with a joystick for traverse and elevation. The ammunition is contained in boxes on the outside of each gun. The former designation was HS 666.

Weight: 1,540kg travelling; 1,200kg firing
Traverse: 360° Rate 80°/sec
Elevation: −3° to +81° Rate 48°/sec
Sight: Galileo P56 computer sight
Status: All the above mountings are in service.

Right: *Oerlikon GAI-DO1 twin mounting.* Above: *Type GAI-CO3*

OERLIKON GUN TURRET TYPE GAD-AOA

(SWITZERLAND)

This armoured, one-man, multi-purpose gun turret is equipped with a single Oerlikon 20mm cannon type KAA (former designation 204GK) details of which are given above. The turret is armour-plated to give protection against small-arms fire and is sealed against chemical and radioactive particle hazards. The cannon itself is mounted outside the turret thus permitting freedom of movement within and preventing the ingress of fumes. The height of the seat and platform can be adjusted to suit the gunner.

Ammunition is belt-fed from the right and the gun can be reloaded with the hatch closed and full armour protection, the last chance to reload with such protection being indicated by a warning lamp on the gunner's forehand support. A large ammunition capacity coupled with these reloading arrangements enable the turret to be kept ready for action over long periods. Gun laying is by handwheel.

The turret is suitable for installation in a variety of armoured vehicles. Known installations are the Mowag Piranha APC and Tornado MICV and the Austrian Saurer APC.

Weight: 1,055kg all up
Traverse: Unlimited
Elevation: −12° to +70°
Manufacturer: Machine Tool Works, Oerlikon Bührle
Status: In production. In service in Austria at least

Gun turret GAD-AOA in Mowag Piranha APC

OERLIKON 20mm NAVAL MOUNTINGS

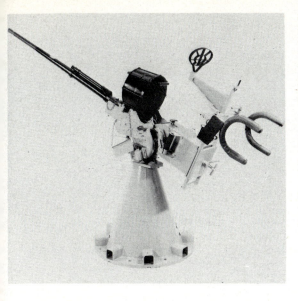

Among the many mountings for the discontinued HSS 804 drum-fed cannon which are still to be found in service in many parts of the world is the A41 naval mounting. This is a simple one-man pedestal mount with a ring and bead sight which can be used for either surface or AA fire. The weight of the mounting, including ammunition is 240kg and it is thus evidently suitable for installation on small or very small naval or riverine craft.

A more modern mounting using the belt-fed KAA cannon is the GAM-B. This too has a ring and bead sight and is laid by the gunner using a shoulder harness: elevation limits are −15 to +60 degrees and traverse is unlimited. All-up weight with 200 rounds of ammunition is about 500kg.

Status: Both mountings are in service and the GAM-B is currently produced by Oerlikon in Zurich and British Manufacture and Research Co. in the UK.

A41A Hispano-Oerlikon naval mounting

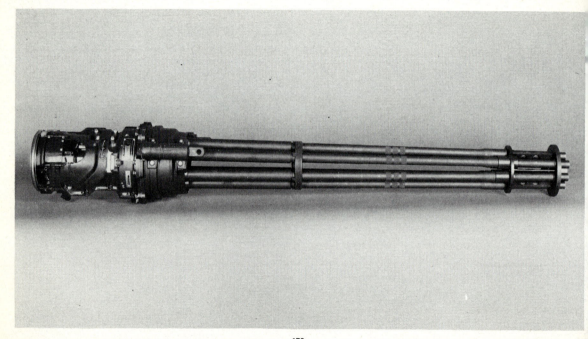

This is a modified form of the M61A1 airborne weapon. Like the M61A1 it is externally powered and has a cluster of six barrels. The rate of fire has been modified from the 6,000 rounds/minute of the M61A1 and the M168 is capable of firing at 1,000 or 3,000 rounds/minute. The gun is basically a Gatling type mechanism in which each of the six barrels fires only once during each revolution of the barrel cluster. Barrels are attached to the gun rotor by interrupted threads and no headspace adjustment is required. The muzzles are held in a muzzle clamp which allows the dispersion of shot to be spread into a flattened ellipse. The gun rotor rests on bearings inside the stationary outer housing and contains the six gun bolts. As the bolts rotate around the rotor, a cam follower on each bolt follows a stationary cam path fixed to the housing and this causes the bolt to reciprocate and carry out the functions of feeding, chambering, locking, firing, unlocking, and extraction. Since each barrel only fires once for each revolution i.e. 500 rounds/minute/barrel, there is no chance of cook off. Any misfires are thrown out of the gun (and so are hangfires). When the gun stops firing, the bolts are held back and so the chambers are left empty. Alternatively a declutching feeder can be used which permits firing of all ammunition actually in the gun. The gun weighs 136kg and

M61A1 six-barrelled gun

the weight of mounting, ammunition etc. varies with the carriage.

Manufacturer: Aircraft Equipment Division, General Electric (USA)
Status: In production and in service

Applications
Three versions of a land force mobile AA system based on this gun have been developed in the USA. The first two — the M163 and M167 Vulcan Air Defence Systems — differ mainly in that the M163 is a SP system mounted on a modified M113 APC whereas the M167 is a towed system on a two-wheel trailer. Both are equipped with a ranging radar which supplies range and range-rate data to a lead-computing sight system which is used by the gunner to track and engage the target.

The third system is known as the Autotrack Vulcan Air Defence System (AVADS). This incorporates some general design improvements over the earlier systems but the important changes are the replacement of the range-only radar by one that will also track the target in angle, the incorporation of an improved fire-control computer and the introduction of a helmet-mounted sight. The gunner acquires the target by turning his head towards it and locating it in his helmet sight reticle: as he does so the radar antenna reproduces his head motion and, when the

gunner — having acquired the target — operates a trigger, starts to transmit and acquires and tracks the target electronically. Using data from the radar, the fire control computer then directs the turret to the appropriate azimuth, lays the gun with the appropriate lead angle and causes it to open fire when the target is within range, firing 2-second bursts until the gunner releases the trigger, whereupon control is returned to the helmet sight.

Data are given below for the AVADS system with notes relating to the earlier systems.

Ammunition: 20mm M50 series
Gun operation: Externally powered Gatling principle. Automatic
Feed: Linked or linkless
Gun Weight: 136kg
System weight: 2,363kg AVADS and M163: 1,500kg M167
Traverse: Unlimited
Elevation: −5° to +80°
Traverse rate: 80°/sec (M163 and M167 60°/sec)
Elevation rate: 60°/sec (M163 and M167 45°/sec)
Rate of fire: 1,000 or 3,000 rounds/min
Sight: Helmet-mounted (M163 and M167, M61 lead-computing)
Manufacturer: Gun and system, General Electric (USA)
Status: M163/167 in service in the USA and Israel: AVADS not yet adopted. The gun is also used in the fully-automatic naval close-in weapon system known as Vulcan/Phalanx and two visually-controlled mountings are made by GE (USA) for installation on naval vessels

Left: *M167 Vulcan AA system.* Above: *AVADS-Autotrack Vulcan Air Defence System*

M197 GUN

This is an externally-powered lightweight version of the M61A1 Vulcan gun and is similar in its operation to the M168 (qv) except that it has only three barrels instead of six. Its present service use is in airborne applications only but it can readily be pintle-mounted for land vehicle use and a naval mounting for light vessels has been developed using a Mk 10 gun mount. A 30mm (3-barrel) version, designated XM-188, is in development for helicopter applications but also has land force potential.

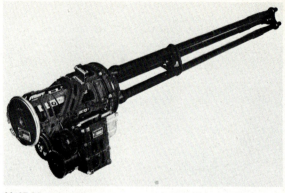

M197 20 mm gun

Ammunition: 20mm M50 series (M197): (30mm XM552 HEDP for XM-188)
Operation: Externally powered Gatling type with 3 barrels
Feed: Linked or linkless
Weight: Gun 66.5kg; Barrel 8.2kg (XM-188 varies according to barrel length)
Length: 183cm; Barrel 152.5cm (XM-188 147.5cm or 178cm with 106.5 or 137cm barrels)
Rate of fire: 400-1,500 rounds/min (XM-188 400-2,000 rounds/min)
Manufacturer: General Electric (USA)
Status: M 197 production for US, Iranian and Korean forces for airborne applications. XM-188 in development. No known land service commitment for either.

Cannon-armed V-150 Commando APC

Several vehicle mountings for 20mm cannon have been developed in the USA, the weapons commonly, but not necessarily, being the M139 licence-built version of the HS 820 (Oerlikon KAD) made in the US ordnance factories. This weapon is found, for example, on one version of the M114 command and reconnaissance carrier.

A more elaborate 20mm mounting is that for the Commando V-150 APC. This is a turret incorporating a 7.62mm MG mounted coaxially with the cannon and with a further MG on the turret roof for AA defence. The turret is powered by a Cadillac Gage electrohydraulic traverse and elevation system providing unlimited traverse and gun elevation between −8 and +60 degrees. The V-150 Commando is made by the Cadillac Gage Company, and is in widespread service.

M1955 TRIPLE CANNON MOUNTING

(YUGOSLAVIA)

Based on the Hispano-Suiza (now Oerlikon) HSS 804 cannon design this is a triple-barrelled weapon designed in Yugoslavia and manufactured there since 1955. It is extensively deployed in the Yugoslav Army and a version of it is used on many of the country's smaller naval vessels. The three barrels are fed by drum magazines and the weapon may be fired either on its two-wheel carriage or, with the wheels raised, from a tripod mount.

Ammunition: 20mm HS
Operation: Blowback with positive breech locking: automatic
Feed: Three 60-round drum magazines
Barrel: 70 calibres
Weight: About 1,200kg all up
Traverse: Unlimited
Elevation: −5° to +85°
Rate of fire: 800 rounds/barrel/minute cyclic
Status: In service with Yugoslav forces.

Triple cannon mounting in service in Yugoslavia

23mm and 25mm CALIBRE WEAPONS

25mm AUTOMATIC CANNON TYPE KBA-B

This gun was based on the 25mm cannon produced in the USA by Thompson, Ramo, Wooldridge (TRW). The original concept was designed by Eugene Stoner and incorporated the rotating bolt lock which is a feature of his smaller calibre M 16 Rifle. The US weapon was originated in 1964 for the Bushmaster trials but was also tested extensively throughout Europe. It was known as the TRW 6425 and was the first gun to incorporate a dual feed system. When the Bushmaster programme was postponed during the Vietnam War the European patent rights were taken up by Oerlikon. Further development work was carried out and the gun was modified from recoil to gas operation.

In its modified form the gun resembles the 20mm Hispano/Oerlikon series in that blowback is used to eject the spent cartridge case and impart additional energy to the bolt on its rearward stroke. Gas vented from the barrel operates a short-stroke piston to drive the bolt carrier to the rear and a cam on the carrier both unlocks the bolt and provides some rearward impetus to which the blowback action is added. Before unlocking the bolt and barrel recoil about 25-30mm, thus reducing the trunnion pull.

The two ammunition belts are fed up on each side of the receiver and are linked so that when one side is feeding the other is free. By switching the linkage the gunner can change rapidly from one type of ammunition to the other.

Ammunition: 25mm
Operation: Semi-blowback with positive breech locking and gas unlocking. Selective fire
Feed: Dual selective belt. Feed from below
Weight: Gun 108kg; Barrel 37kg
Length: Gun 280.5cm; Barrel 217.5cm, 80 calibres
Rate of fire: 570 rounds/min
Manufacturer: Machine Tool Works Oerlikon Bührle
Status: In production and in service.

Oerlikon KBA-B cannon

25mm AUTOMATIC CANNON TYPE KBA-CO1

(SWITZERLAND)

This gun operates in the same way as the KBA-B. It is a gas operated gun with a recoiling barrel to reduce the trunnion pull. It differs from the KBA-B in that it is intended to be used with a ground mount and with such a mount the dual feed takes the ammunition in from the top.

Ammunition: 25mm
Operation: Semi-blowback with positive breech locking. Selective fire
Feed: Dual selective belt. Feed from above
Weight: Gun 109kg; Barrel 38kg
Length: Gun 291.5cm; Barrel 218cm, 80 calibres
Rate of fire: 600 rounds/min
Manufacturer: Machine Tool Works Oerlikon Bührle
Status: In production and in service.

Automatic cannon type KBA-CO1

(SWITZERLAND)

25mm OERLIKON MOUNTING TYPE GBI

GBI mounting for the KBA-CO1

This infantry mounting incorporates the 25mm KBA-CO1 cannon (qv). The mount is a tripod, giving all-round traverse and an elevation range from −10 to +70 degrees, which is mounted on a two-wheel trailer. The gun is traversed by a handwheel, which can be declutched to give a free swing and elevated by a second handwheel. A box containing 40 rounds of belted ammunition is mounted on each side of the gun which is fed from both sides. The gun is served by a three-man crew and can be fired off its wheels in an emergency. The mount can be broken down into convenient loads for transport over difficult terrain.

Weight: Travelling 550kg; Firing 410kg
Traverse: Unlimited
Elevation: −10° to +70°
Ammunition Supply: 2 × 40 rounds
Manufacturer: Oerlikon Bührle
Status: In production and in service.

25mm OERLIKON TURRET TYPE GBD

Oerlikon have developed a series of turret mountings, for the 25mm KBA-B cannon, under the general designation GBD. They are one-man power-operated mountings suitable for installation on a variety of armoured vehicles, known installations being on one version of the US Lynx Command and Reconnaissance Vehicle supplied by FMC to the Netherlands (GBD-AO5), on a version of the M113 APC (GBD-B20) and on the Mowag Tornado APC. The turrets are equipped with periscopic day sights for engaging ground and air targets, periscopic night sights and additional periscopes for observation and a coaxial MG can be fitted to the main gun armature. Typical data are given below but there are variations in weight and elevation angle between the three installations and options exist for at least emergency manual control and turret stabilisation

Weight: 940kg; 1,055kg with ammunition
Traverse: 360°; Rate 70°/sec
Elevation: −15° to +55°
Day sight: ×6 or × 2
Night sight: Infra-red × 4
Manufacturer (Turret and gun): Oerlikon Bührle
Status: In service

Far left: *Oerlikon mounting on Mowag Tornado.* Left: *GBD-A05 mounting on Dutch Command and Reconnaissance vehicle*

23mm ZU-23 CANNON   (USSR)

This is a gas-operated weapon with a long-stroke piston and a vertically-moving breech-block locking system. The breech-block drops to unlock and is raised and lowered in guideways in the body of the gun by the action of cams on the piston extension: cartridges are rammed and spent cases extracted by a separate rammer and extractor, primary extraction resulting from the small rearward motion of the breech-block — which is coupled to the rammer/extractor — as it makes its initial downward movement.

The gun can be fed from either side, a small modification being needed to effect the changeover. A last-round mechanism ensures that the last round in the belt is left on the feed tray ready for ramming and the gun left with the working parts to the rear so that recocking is not necessary when a new belt is fitted.

In its towed mounting the gun is air-cooled but barrels can be changed quickly when hot. In the ZSU-23-4 mounting the guns are water cooled. Both mountings are described further below.

Ammunition: 23mm × 236
Operation: Gas with vertically-moving breech-block locking. Automatic
Feed: Disintegrating-link belt
Weight: Gun 75kg; Barrel 27.2kg
Length: Gun 255.5cm; Barrel 188cm
Rate of fire: 800-1,000 rounds/min
Effective range: 2,500m against ground targets; 1,500m against air targets; Maxima 7,000m and 5,000m
Status: Widely used by Russian, allied and client forces. Presumably still in production.

ZU-23 TWIN TOWED MOUNTING

ZU-23 twin towed mounting in firing position

The ZU-23 is commonly to be found in a twin towed mounting on a light two-wheel carriage. In the firing position the mounting, which is provided with jacks, rests on the ground with its wheels folded almost flat. Ammunition is carried in 50-round boxes on either side of the guns.

Weight: 950kg all up
Traverse: 360°
Elevation: −10° to +90°
Sights: Optical
Ammunition supply: 2 × 50-round boxes
Status: In service with Warsaw Pact forces and in Cuba, Egypt, Iran, Iraq, Libya, Pakistan, Syria and Vietnam and probably now in several more African countries.

In service with the Russian Army since 1965, the ZSU-23-4 self-propelled AA gun system, also known as the Shilka, has been made in large numbers and supplied to many countries outside Russia. The armament comprises four 23mm ZU-23 cannon in a water-cooled version and the vehicle is equipped with a combined target acquisition and fire-control radar, known as the B-26 or by the NATO code-name Gun Dish, and a fire-control computer. The radar is said to have a range of 20km. Optical sights are fitted for use against both ground and air targets.

Guns, radar, computer and ammunition are installed in a large, powered turret mounted on a modified PT-76 light tank chassis and the system can be operated while on the move. Comparison of early models in Russian Army service with more recent models reveals some minor external differences in turret design but the significance of these is not known. The operational capabilities of the system were clearly demonstrated in the 1973 Arab-Israeli war when it was used to considerable effect against Israeli aircraft.

Crew: 4
Weight: 14 tonnes complete
Turret traverse: 360°
Gun elevation: $-7°$ to $+80°$
Gun control: Radar or optical
Rate of fire: 800-1,000 rounds/barrel/min cyclic: 200 rounds/barrel/min practical
Ammunition supply: 500 rounds/barrel
Status: In production and in service in most Warsaw Pact countries and in Angola, Egypt, Finland, India, Iran, Iraq, Syria and Yemen at least

ZSU-23-4 in service in Egypt (SIPA)

Several twin mountings for 25mm light AA guns are to be found in Russian naval vessels and on ships of client navies. The more modern mountings are enclosed: earlier vessels had open or semi-enclosed installations. The guns are recoil operated. Data are given below for the gun mounting Type 2-M-3 110PM which is a local control mounting with visual sighting and powered laying with manual standby.

Ammunition: 25mm
Weight: 1,500kg
Length: 285cm total; Barrel 80 calibres
Traverse: 360°; Rates 70°/sec or 25°/sec manual
Elevation: −10° to +85°; Rates 40°/sec or 15°/sec manual
Rate of fire: 270-300 rounds/min cyclic
Crew: 2
Status: In service

Enclosed 25 mm naval AA mounting

25mm BUSHMASTER CANNON

Bushmaster is the name given to a cannon which will arm the new US XM723 MICV. A final decision on the design of the weapon will be taken as a result of competitive trials of two 25mm weapons.

The competing weapons are an Americanized version of the gas-operated Oerlikon KBA cannon (qv) which has been developed by Ford Aerospace and Ammunition Corporation and the 25mm XM242 Chain Gun developed by Hughes and described below

According to the latest known programme the Bushmaster is expected to be introduced into the MICV production line at around the 300th model late in 1980, replacing the interim M139 20mm cannon — which is the US copy of the Oerlikon KAD (qv).

Manufacturers: Ford Aerospace and Communications Corporation (formerly Aeronutronic Ford) and Hughes Helicopters and Ordnance Systems
Status: Competitive evaluation.

25mm CHAIN GUN XM242

Currently under development by Hughes Helicopters and Ordnance Systems this dual-feed 25mm version of their 30mm Chain Gun (qv) is the subject of a US Army contract calling for the delivery of 23 prototype models, the first of which is scheduled for February 1978. By mid-1977 15,000 rounds had been fired by two test weapons at the Hughes plant.

Apart from its calibre and consequent dimensional changes the XM242 differs from the larger weapon in the fire modes available. It can fire either semi-automatically (single shots) or automatically with selectable rates of fire of 100, 200 and 550 rounds per minute.

The XM242 is one of two contenders for the US Bushmaster contract for the armament of the XM723 MICV.

Ammunition: 25mm XM 790 and Oerlikon KBA
Operation: Externally powered and controlled mechanism. Selective fire (see text)
Feed: Dual disintegrating-link belt
Weight: 95.3kg; Barrel 36.3kg
Length: 274.5cm; Barrel 203cm
Rate of fire: Single shots or 100-550 rounds/min (see text)
Manufacturer: Hughes Helicopters and Ordnance Systems
Status: Development (see text)

25mm AIFV TURRET MOUNTING

(USA)

FMC Armoured Infantry Fighting Vehicles (AIFV) being delivered to the Netherlands are armed with an Oerlikon KBA 25mm cannon and a coaxial 7.62mm FN MAG MG in a turret mounting. The turret has an electro-hydraulic laying mechanism with emergency manual control, can be fitted with an add-on electro-hydraulic stabilisation system and is adaptable to other kinds of armament. Operated by one man, the turret is fitted with a Philips day/night sight ($\times$ 2 and $\times$ 6), an open emergency AA sight and four M27 periscopes for observation. A 150W infra-red/white searchlight is coupled to the armature of the 35mm cannon.

Traverse: 360°; Rate 45°/sec
Elevation: $-10°$ to $+55°$; Rate 60°/sec
Ammunition Supply: 165 rounds 25mm; 230 rounds 7.62mm
Vehicle Manufacturer: FMC Corporation, San Jose, California
Status: In production. Deliveries to Netherlands scheduled 1977/78

30mm CALIBRE WEAPONS

Note. While the weapons described in this division are all of 30mm calibre they do not all use the same ammunition.

Reference should be made to the 20mm entries for details of the Spanish Meroka multi-gun system.

Brief details of the US XM-188 3-barrel 30mm gun will be found in the entry for the M197 20mm gun.

(CZECHOSLOVAKIA)

Two versions of a twin 30mm AA mounting are in service in Czechoslovakia. The M-53 is an open mounting on a light four-wheel trailer: the M-59 is a partially enclosed mounting, giving the gunner some protection, installed on an armoured version of the Praga 6×6 V3S truck.

The 30mm cannon are gas-operated and magazine-fed (M-59) or clip-fed (M-53) and fire both HE and API rounds. The magazines for the M-59 are mounted vertically on the top of the guns while the clips for the M-53 are fed horizontally. Early models had multi-baffle muzzle brakes but these have been replaced on later models by conical flash eliminators. The barrels are easily changed. Gunlaying is hydraulically powered.

Ammunition: 30mm (.9kg round; .45kg projectile)
Operation: Gas
Feed: 10-round clip (M-53) or 50-round box magazine (M-59)
Firing weight: Mounting 2,000kg
Traverse: 360°
Elevation: −10° to +90°
Sights: Optical
Rate of fire: 450-500/rounds/min/barrel cyclic; 100-150 rounds/min/barrel practical
Range: 2,000m practical. Maximum about 10,000m
Status: In service in Czechoslovakia.

Mounted on either an AMX-13 or an AMX-30 chassis to form the AMX-13 DCA or AMX-30 DCA respectively, this SAMM turret mounting for twin 30mm cannon is an important item in the French AA systems inventory. The turret is electro-hydraulically powered and carries a Thomson-CSF Oeil Vert surveillance and track-while-scan ranging radar. The guns are Oerlikon KCB cannon (formerly designated HSS 831A).

The Oeil Vert is a coherent doppler pulse radar providing omnidirectional surveillance (15km on a 3 sq m target up to 3,000m altitude) during the search phase and ranging up to 10km during the firing phase. The two sets of data are fed continuously to the turret for target designation by the commander and fire-control aim correction respectively. Commander and gunner are equipped with SAGEM sights with aim correction by rotating mirrors for AA fire and with APX M250 episcope sights for ground fire. There are also eight episcopes for observation.

Traverse: 360°; Rate 80°/sec
Elevation: −8° to +85°; Rate 45°/sec
Ammunition Supply: 600 rounds/gun
Manufacturer: SAMM, 224 quai Stalingrad — 92130 Issy-les-Moulineux (turret). System supplier GIAT
Status: AMX-13 DCA in service with the French Army and production complete. AMX-30 DCA in production.

AMX-30 DCA system with TGA 230A twin turret on AMX-30 chassis

OERLIKON KCB CANNON

(SWITZERLAND)

Formerly known as the HSS 831 the weapon now known as the KCB is a 30mm cannon which in most respects is a scaled-up version of the KAB (formerly HS 820) 20mm weapon and has the same principle of operation. It is fed either by a clip-feed mechanism containing eight clips of five rounds each or by a left-hand or right-hand belt feed.

Ammunition: 30mm
Operation: Blowback with positive breech locking. Automatic
Feed: 8 × 5-round clips or belt
Weight: 136kg; Barrel 61kg
Length: 357cm; Barrel 260cm, 75 calibres
Rate of fire: 600-650 rounds/min
Manufacturer: Machine Tool Works Oerlikon Bührle
Status: In production and in service

Oerlikon 30 mm KCB cannon

Formerly known as the HS 661, this towed mounting is designed for use with the Oerlikon KCB cannon (qv) and is suitable for the engagement of both ground and air targets. It is towed on a two-wheel trailer and lowered to the ground for firing.

Gunlaying is hydraulic, controlled by a joystick, with mechanical fallback and the mounting is equipped with a Galileo P36 (mechanical) or P56 (electronic) computer sight. Ammunition is fed from a box containing eight clips of five rounds each. Power is supplied by a small petrol-electric generator on the mount.

Weight: 1,540kg travelling; 1,150kg firing
Length: 540cm travelling; 515cm firing
Traverse: 360°; Rate 110°/sec
Elevation: $-3°$ to $+81°$ hydraulic; Rate 60°/sec; $-5°$ to $+83°$ mechanical
Ammunition supply: 40 rounds on the gun

Designed specifically for AFV applications the Rarden 30mm cannon is a light, accurate, primarily anti-armour weapon having a short inboard length, a low trunnion pull and low toxicity. It is unusual in having a long-recoil operating mechanism (which reduces the recoil forces and toxicity) in which the breech remains locked for two-thirds of the 33cm recoil motion (by which time the pressure in the barrel is down to atmospheric), the final third being used to open the breech and make the primary extraction of the spent case. This is left on the rammer as the barrel moves forward and after some 20cm of run-out the case is ejected and a new round taken from the feed mechanism for ramming.

This arrangement results in a relatively low rate of fire but this in turn contributes to the accuracy of the weapon since there is less residual vibration in the system when the next round is fired than there would be with a shorter cycle. The feed mechanism takes two three-round clips of ammunition.

Ammunition: 30mm special APDS APSE and HE and standard HS 831L
Operation: Long recoil. Selective fire
Feed: 2 × 3-round clips
Weight: Gun 95.3kg; Barrel 24.5kg
Length: 296cm; Barrel 244cm
Rate of fire: Approx 90 rounds/min cyclic
Manufacturer: RSAF, Enfield
Status: In service with British, Belgian and Nigerian Armies

RARDEN cannon

RARDEN TURRET FOR FOX CVR

This is a two-man turret armed with a Rarden 30mm gun and a coaxial 7.62mm MG. Developed for use on the Fox armoured car it can also be installed on a modified FV 432 APC and in this form it is used by Mechanised Infantry Battalions of the British Army.

Gunlaying is by a power-assisted manual system and the weapons are electrically fired with manual standby. For normal operations the commander acts also as loader while the gunner aims and fires; but if necessary one man can fight the turret. Both commander and gunner have a periscope binocular ($\times 1$ and $\times 10$) and there is an image-intensifier night sight, L2A1, which has two operating modes, $\times 5.8$ with an 8-degree field and $\times 1.6$ with a 28-degree field, the latter being used for surveillance. The commander has seven observation periscopes and the gunner two. Gun elevation limits are from -14 to $+41$ degrees — making it possible to engage helicopter targets — but the Rarden gun is primarily a weapon for use against ground targets.

Vehicle manufacturer: Royal Ordnance Factory, Leeds
Status: In production and in service in the UK, Iran, Nigeria and Saudi Arabia

Fox armoured reconnaissance vehicle with Rarden turret (UK MOD)

(UNITED KINGDOM)

RARDEN TURRET FOR SCIMITAR CVR (T) FV107

This turret is very similar to that mounted on the Fox armoured car and has the same armament and sighting and observation equipment. Gunlaying for vehicles in service is manual but a powered system has been developed.

Vehicle manufacturer: British Leyland Ltd. (Alvis), Coventry. Also made in Belgium.
Status: In production and in service in the British Army

FV107 Scimitar CVR with Rarden turret

The Falcon mobile AA system was a joint development by Vickers Ltd and the British Manufacture and Research Co. It consists of a turret mounting two 30mm Oerlikon KCB cannon (formerly HSS 831L) installed on a modified Abbot gun chassis. The two-man turret has power elevation and traverse and the weapons are stabilised so that they can be fired while the vehicle is moving. Both commander and gunner are provided with periscope day sights ($\times$ 1 and $\times$ 6), the gunner's $\times$ 1 sight having an automatic lead angle display for AA fire, and the commander has two observation periscopes.

The guns are cocked and fired electrically and can be fired independently or together with a choice of single shots or automatic fire. The gunner controls the movement of the turret and guns using a joystick which is energised by a foot pedal.

Traverse: 360°; Rate 80°/sec (slew) or 45°/sec (tracking)
Elevation: $-10°$ to $+85°$; Rate 40°/sec
Ammunition supply: 620 rounds
Vehicle manufacturer: Vickers Ltd.
Status: Private venture development to completion of trials.

Falcon AA vehicle

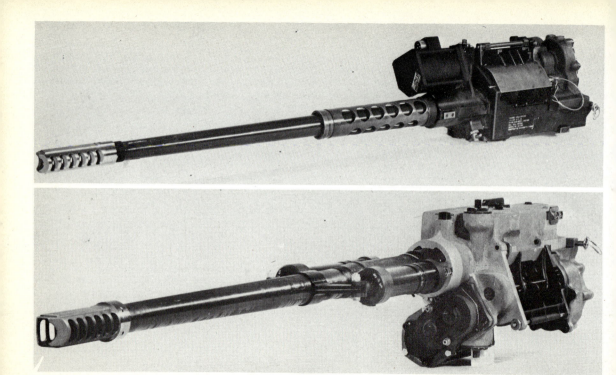

212

XM230 CHAIN GUN

Developed by Hughes Helicopters and Ordnance Systems, the 30mm XM230 Chain Gun is a single barrel externally powered weapon which incorporates a rotating bolt mechanism driven by a simple chain drive. The gun fires from an open breech and has a variable rate of fire up to 800 rounds a minute. It was originally intended for the US Army Advanced Attack Helicopter and is now considered to be suitable for use on US Army ground vehicles.

In a chain gun system, since all moving parts are strictly mechanically related, all mechanical operations are closely timed and controlled. It is thus possible to use a single operational cycle without sacrifice of safety and with considerable savings in manufacturing cost. Furthermore, the gun function is independent of ammunition ballistics: this means not only that the rate of fire can be varied at will within wide limits but also that the number of highly stressed components is small: the receiver function is limited to ammunition handling and the receiver itself experiences no loads resulting from chamber pressure or buffer impacts.

The basic mechanism provides for either forward or side ejection and is readily modified to incorporate a dual feeder. The bolt lock time is relatively long (up to 20 milliseconds) and this means that gas efflux from the breech is negligible and the risk of a hangfire accident virtually eliminated.

Firing to date has been with XM639 ammunition, one of the WECOM 30 family. Because the US Army is considering a change to the XM788/789 family which will be interoperable with the European 30mm ADEN/DEFA ammunition, Hughes are modifying their design accordingly: this involves a small increase in weapon size over the figures given below for the current ammunition.

Ammunition: 30mm XM-552/639 dual-purpose (see text)
Operation: Externally powered and controlled mechanism. Variable rate of fire
Feed: Disintegrating-link belt
Weight: 27.2kg; Barrel 13.6kg
Length: 160cm; Barrel 106.5cm
Rate of fire: Variable 1-800 rounds/min; Normal 620 rounds/min
Effective range: 3,000m
Manufacturer: Hughes Helicopters and Ordnance Systems
Status: Developed.

Top: *XM230 chain gun—basic pattern.* Below: *XM230—linkless ammunition version*

35mm and 37mm CALIBRE WEAPONS

Originating in a development to meet a German Army requirement in the 1960s two mobile AA systems, mounted on Leopard Tank chassis and armed with the Oerlikon 35mm gun are currently in production, one having been ordered for Belgium and West Germany and the other for the Netherlands. The first is known as the 5PZF-B or Gepard and the second as the 5PZF-C or Cheetah.

The turrets of the two systems are similar in many respects but the Gepard has separate surveillance and tracking radars, by Siemens (Munich) and Siemens-Albis (Zurich) respectively, while the Cheetah has an integrated search and tracking radar system by Hollandse Signaalapparaten (Netherlands).

The turret is in each case powered and operated by two men. In addition to the radar antennae mounted fore and aft it is equipped with a fire-control computer which not only corrects the aim of the guns for target distance and speed, gun muzzle velocity and so forth but also controls the rate of fire as a function of target range. The search and tracking radars of the Gepard and the Cheetah differ not only in type but also in transmitter frequency but they both have operational ranges in the region of 15km — well beyond the practical engagement range of the guns which is about 4km.

In addition to the radar surveillance and target tracking system each crew member has a stabilised panoramic telescope which can be used for observation, visual target acquisition and aiming at ground targets.

A dual ammunition feed is provided for each gun. AA ammunition is carried within the turret in belts and a smaller quantity of anti-tank ammunition is carried externally in armoured boxes. The gunner can switch quickly from one type to the other and each gun can fire single shots or bursts or automatically.

Traverse: Unlimited; Rates 90°/sec (slewing); 56°/sec (tracking)
Elevation: −5° to +85°; Rate 42°/sec
Feed: Dual with belted AA and boxed ATk
Ammunition Supply: 330 rounds/gun AA; 20 rounds/gun ATk
Vehicle Manufacturer: Krauss-Maffei AG, Munich
Status: Both versions are in production, the Gepard for West Germany and Belgium and the Cheetah for the Netherlands.

5PZF-B (Gepard) mobile AA system

35mm OERLIKON KDC (AND TOWED TWIN MOUNTING)

Like the smaller Oerlikon (Hispano) cannon the Oerlikon 35mm automatic gun type KDC is gas operated with positive breech locking. The barrel and gun body move rearwards on the cradle slides during recoil, the gun cover and feed mechanism remaining stationary, and the gun fires during the counter-recoil movement. This 'floating firing' action reduces the recoil forces and these are further reduced by the provision of a muzzle brake — to which is secured a muzzle velocity measuring device which is used to correct the ballistic data in an associated fire-control computer.

A standard mounting for the gun is a four-wheel trailer GDF-001 carrying two KDC guns. To bring the guns into action the wheels are folded upwards, lowering the platform supports to the ground, and the platform is then levelled automatically within seven degrees by remote control. In this way the gun can be brought into action in 90 seconds by two men or 150 seconds by one. The operation can also be performed manually.

Ammunition for the guns is held in 56-round hoppers which can be recharged, while the guns are firing if necessary, with seven-round clips. Including the rounds in the hoppers, 238 rounds are carried on the mounting. Gunlaying is electrically powered and controlled either remotely

Oerlikon type GDF twin 35 mm AA mounting

or locally by joystick and there is an emergency manual laying facility. The mounting is normally associated with a radar and computer fire-control system, such as the Contraves Super-Fledermaus: for local control there is an AA sight and a telescope for the engagement of ground targets.

Ammunition: 35mm Oerlikon
Operation: Gas operated with positive locking. Selective fire
Feed: Hopper and 7-round clips (a belt feed is used in some other mountings)
Weight: Twin mounting without ammunition 6,000kg; 6,400kg with 238 rounds
Length: 7.9m travelling; Barrel 315cm, 90 calibres
Width: 2.3m travelling
Traverse: Unlimited; Rate 120°/sec
Elevation: −5° to +92°; Rate 60°/sec
Rate of fire: 550 rounds/barrel/min cyclic
Effective range: 4,000m
Penetration: 44mm at 1,000m
Ammunition Supply: 56 rounds/gun plus 63 rounds/gun on the mounting
Manufacturer: Machine Tool Works Oerlikon Bührle
Status: In production and in service in Switzerland and at least 10 other countries.

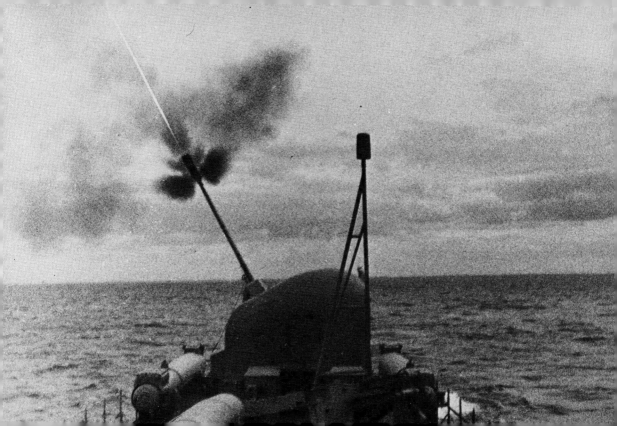

35mm (OERLIKON) NAVAL MOUNTINGS

Oerlikon 35mm guns are well suited to the roles of principal armament on light naval craft or secondary — mainly AA — armament on larger vessels. A mounting which is particularly appropriate to the latter role is the Oerlikon (Switzerland) twin mounting type GDM-A which can be either remotely controlled by a radar or optical fire-control system or locally electrically controlled using a gyro-stabilised sight with emergency fully-manual operation.

Another twin mounting is the OE/OTO by Oerlikon Italiana and Oto Melara in Italy. It has the same control options as the GDM-A and is unusual in that both guns have dual belt feeds enabling the gunner to switch from one type of ammunition to another in about two seconds.

Status: In production and in service

Left: *Oerlikon twin naval mounting GDM-A.* Above: *OE/OTO twin naval mounting*

Above: *M1939 LAA gun* (Novosti)

Right: *Twin 37 mm mounting in service in Laos*

This gun is a modified version of the M-1938 light anti-aircraft gun which in turn was based on the Swedish 40mm Bofors design. Apart from the difference in calibre it

resembles American and British Bofors-type guns of the same period. Recoil-operated with a rising breech mechanism it is fed with five-round clips of ammunition from the top. The standard army mounting is on a four-wheel trailer from which it is brought into action by levelling the platform on four jacks (two on outriggers) and removing the wheels. All operations are manual. It is no longer in first-line service in the USSR, having been replaced by the 57mm M-1960 gun (qv) and other AA weapons, but is still to be found in large numbers in the armies of client countries. It is known (and made) in China as the 37mm Type 55.

Ammunition: 37mm HE-T, AP-T, HVAP-T
Operation: Recoil
Feed: 5-round clips
Weight: About 2,000kg on 4-wheel trailer
Length: 6.2m travelling. Barrel 257.5cm
Width: 1.7m travelling
Traverse: Unlimited
Elevation: −5° to +85°
Rate of fire: 160-180 rounds/min cyclic; 80 rounds/min practical
Range: 8,000m maximum; 1,400m AA
Status: No longer made in USSR. In service in at least fourteen countries outside the USSR. A twin mounting is in service in Albania and China

37mm RUSSIAN NAVAL MOUNTINGS

The M-1939 37mm LAA gun described above appears in single open and turret mountings on many of the older (and mostly small) ships of the Russian Navy. Twin mountings of a more modern water-cooled weapon are also found on many ships of similar age.

A more modern version of the 37 mm gun in a twin naval mounting (Novosti)

WEAPONS WITH CALIBRES OF 40mm OR MORE

Possibly the most famous gun of the Second World War and used in one form or another by almost all the combatant nations, the 40mm Bofors light AA gun was originated by Bofors in 1928 and, after the Swedish government had given it financial backing, first delivered to the Royal Swedish Navy in 1932. By 1939 Bofors had delivered guns for land or naval use to eighteen countries (excluding colonies) and manufacturing licences had been taken up in ten countries outside Sweden.

The standard wartime model was the M36 which differed from the earliest model in only minor respects. It was recoil-operated, air-cooled and fed by four-round clips of ammunition inserted in a guide on top of the gun casing. Gunlaying was manual by two men sitting on either side of the gun and each equipped with ring sights. More elaborate sights and predictors were devised during the war but an experienced crew could produce very good results with the open sights.

For land use the standard mounting was a four-wheel towed carriage with jacks fore and aft and two more on outriggers to make a four-point support, the wheels normally being removed for firing. Given a brick or two to chock the wheels, however, the gun could be — and often was — fired from the carriage at the halt. There were

Single 40/60 mounting on HMS Hubberston (UK MOD)

several versions of this carriage and numerous single and twin naval mountings.

In 1942 the version of the gun generally known as the L/60 (60 calibre barrel) was introduced and was very widely adopted by both land and naval forces during the post-war years. It is no longer produced by Bofors, having been superseded by the L/70 weapon (qv) but in both Swedish and licence-built versions it is still in widespread service — in both major and minor forces — and reconditioned weapons are frequently fitted in new installations. Many of the older weapons — notably those made in very large numbers during the war in the UK and the USA (as the M1) — are also still to be found in minor forces. Typical data for the L/60 weapon are given below with some notes relating to the earlier model.

Ammunition: 40mm
Operation: Recoil
Feed: 4-round clips
Weight: 1,730kg in combat order (M36 2,000-2,400kg)
Barrel length: 60 calibres
Traverse: Unlimited
Elevation: $-5°$ to $+90°$
Rate of fire: 120 rounds/min cyclic. Practical about 70
Range: 10.1km maximum (M36 8.7km); AA about 1.2km
Manufacturer: AB Bofors and many others
Status: No longer made in Sweden. Still widely used.

This is a further development of the Bofors LAA gun, the earlier history of which is sketched in the preceding entry. The L/70 has a 70-calibre barrel producing a higher muzzle velocity and hence greater effective range than the L/60: it also has a much higher rate of fire and in the Bofors mountings there is provision for holding up to 16 rounds in a curved magazine above the gun and there are racks for 48 ready rounds at the rear of the standard towed trailer.

The first prototype was produced in 1947 and production started in 1951. Since then it has been produced, in Sweden and elsewhere, with a variety of mounting arrangements for land use and in an even greater diversity of naval mountings. The basic design lends itself readily to operation in association with various fire control systems, power operation and remote control.

An important series of mountings is that developed by Breda Meccanica Bresciana, the Bofors licensees in Italy. The series includes both land and naval (single and twin) mountings and Breda have developed a range of automatic feed systems to go with them. For the army and naval mountings there are 32-round and 144-round feeds and there is an additional 100-round feed for naval use. Breda have also developed a remotely-controlled twin compact mounting (Type 70) which is available in versions having either 444 or 736 rounds in its magazine.

A recent Bofors development is BOFI, an optronic fire-control system which is mounted on the gun and com-

Left: *Bofors 40 mm L/70 AA gun on standard mobile mounting.*
Above: *Arrangement of the Breda/Bofors 144-round magazine and feed*

prises a day/night sight, a laser rangefinder, a computer and a control unit. The system can be used either independently or in conjunction with radar. Introduced in 1972, it is now in production as also is proximity-fused ammunition for the L/70 series.

Mountings for the gun are too numerous to describe in detail here. Listed below are data for a typical Bofors trailer mounting with an integral power unit for gunlaying. The next entry describes a self-propelled version made in the USA.

Ammunition: 40mm point-detonating (self-destructive) or proximity
Operation: Recoil
Feed: Top-fed by various mechanisms
Weight: About 5,000kg on trailer with standard feed and integral power unit
Barrel length: 70 calibres
Traverse: Unlimited, powered or manual. Powered rate 45°/sec
Elevation: −5° to +90°. Powered rate 85°/sec
Rate of fire: 300 rounds/min cyclic
Range: 12.6km maximum; 4km practical
Manufacturer: AB Bofors and others
Status: In widespread army and navy service.

Left: *Men of the RAF Regiment with a 40/70 Bofors during firing practice at Belize International Airport* (UK MOD). Above: *Breda/Bofors 40 mm L/70 AA mounting with 144-round feed*

40mm M42 SP AA GUN

(USA)

This self-propelled twin-gun system, sometimes known as The Duster, was introduced into US Army service in 1953. It comprises two 40mm M2A1 (Bofors-derived) recoil-operated guns in a turret mounted on a tracked vehicle. The turret is power-traversed and the gun can be elevated either manually or with power assistance. Sighting is normally by the M48 (day) computing sight but emergency ring sights are also fitted. The turret has a crew of four men.

Traverse: Unlimited; Rate 40°/sec
Elevation: −3° to +85° (powered) at up to 25°/sec. −5° to +85° manual
Rate of fire: 120 rounds/barrel/min cyclic
Range: About 2,500m ground range with AP ammunition. About 4,000m AA with HE
Vehicle Manufacturer: Most built by Cadillac Division of General Motors
Status: Production complete. In service in Austria, West Germany, Japan, Jordan, Lebanon, Vietnam and (reserve) USA.

M42 twin 40 mm SP AA weapon system (US Army)

57mm M54 AA GUN

(SWEDEN)

This recoil-operated medium AA gun is in service with AA artillery battalions of the Swedish Army and in Belgium where it is made under licence. Its design is generally similar to that of the 40mm Bofors weapons and it is mounted on a similar four-wheel carriage. When in the firing position the wheels are left in place and the platform stabilised by fore and aft and outrigger jacks. The gun is also in service in a naval mounting.

Ammunition: 57mm
Operation: Recoil
Feed: Vertical
Barrel Length: 70 calibres
Weight: 8,100kg in combat order on carriage
Traverse: Unlimited
Elevation: −5° to +90°
Rate of fire: 120 rounds/min cyclic
Range: 14.5km maximum: 4,000m effective AA
Manufacturer: AB Bofors. Also made in Belgium
Status: In service with the Belgian and Swedish Armies.

57/70 naval mounting by Bofors

This widely-used Russian gun is believed to be substantially a copy of one developed, but not put into service, in Germany at the end of the Second World War. It is recoil-operated, has a 73-calibre barrel with a muzzle brake, and for field use it is mounted on a four-wheel carriage from which it can be fired without removing the wheels. A self-propelled version is described separately below. In normal operational use the gun is radar-controlled. The same gun is also to be found in twin and quadruple naval mountings: a single gun mounting found on some of the older Russian ships has no muzzle brake and may differ in other respects; and some more recent remotely-operated twin gun mountings appear to have longer barrels.

Ammunition: 57mm HE/HEI and AP/API with proximity fuse
Operation: Recoil
Feed: Horizontal in 4-round clips
Weight: About 4,000kg on carriage without shield or ready ammunition
Traverse: Unlimited
Elevation: +2° to +87°
Rate of fire: 120 rounds/min cyclic
Range: About 12km maximum; AA 4-6,000m according to fire control system
Status: In service in the USSR and in more than twenty other countries

Left: *Quad-mounted 57 mm Soviet naval guns* (US Naval). Above: *Soviet 57 mm towed AA guns* (Novosti)

57mm ZSU-57-2 SELF-PROPELLED AA SYSTEM (USSR)

This AA vehicle was first seen in 1957 and consists of a twin-gun turret mounted on a modified T-54 tank chassis. The turret holds five men and is armed with two 57mm AA guns which are essentially similar to the S-60 towed gun (qv) and fire the same ammunition. The turret is power-operated with emergency manual standby, the guns hav-ing elevation limits of −5 and +85 degrees. Optical day sights only are fitted.

Status: Production is believed to be complete and the vehicles are in service in fifteen countries including the USSR.

ZSU-23-4 AA weapon system followed by 57 mm ZSu-57-2 twin SP AA guns

INDEX

238